D0898762

Front-Page Women Journalists, 1920-1950

Front-Page

Kathleen A. Cairns

Women

Journalists,

1920-1950

University of Nebraska Press

Lincoln and London

Cataloging-in-Publication Data available
Library of Congress Control Number: 2002031959
ISBN 0-8032-1525-8 (cl.: alkaline paper)
ISBN 978-0-8032-2229-8 (pa: alkaline paper)

For Larry   *In memory of my mother*

Contents

ILLUSTRATIONS

Acknowledgments

My mentors, colleagues, friends, and family saw me through the long process of writing this book, kept me (mostly) sane, and deserve far more thanks than I have space to give them.

At the University of California, Davis, where the project started as my dissertation, scholars who were passionate about the study of history helped me to take a variety of threads, of different colors and textures, and weave them into a single piece of fabric. First and foremost, I owe an immense debt of gratitude to Vicki Ruiz, who encouraged me, set me on the path toward Charlotta Bass, and has become a wonderful friend, as well as mentor.

My pleasure at having finally finished the book is tempered by sadness that two men who offered indispensable counsel at the beginning did not live to see the end product. Roland Marchand opened the door to Ruth Finney's papers. He was a true scholar and a gentleman, never too busy to take time from his own work as a prominent historian of media and popular culture to drop a note saying, "thought you might be able to use this," or to read the latest draft of my work. Paul Goodman, the most honest and demanding critic I have ever had, pushed me far beyond where I thought I could go and taught me to never stop asking the tough questions. Michael Smith also provided some keen insights and showed me that university teaching can be a high art.

This project could not have been completed without the help of archival librarians devoted to keeping alive the words and images of the women on whom this book is centered. At the Southern California Library for Social Studies and Research, I thank Sarah Cooper and Mary Tyler; at the California State University, Northridge, Urban Archives, Robert Marshall; and at the University of California, Davis, Special Collections Department, John Skarstad and Pam Pogojeff.

I also wish to thank generous colleagues who, from the beginning of my career, have made coming to work so much fun. In Long Beach, California, where I spent a decade as a newspaper reporter, I offer gratitude to Mike Schwartz, Joyce Christensen, Rich Archbold, and Larry Allison. At California State University, where I teach history and humanities, I thank George Craft, Henry Chambers, and Jackie Donath.

During the years that this book was coming to be, friends listened patiently as I endlessly propounded upon "my women" and what their lives meant to history. Now that the book is done, I can thank them in print: Kathryn Olmsted, Bill Ainsworth, Dorothy Korber, Susan Pack, Dennis McDougal, Sue Pearson Atkinson, Mark Gladstone, Felecia Keys, Annette Reed, Yolanda Wallace, Margaret Jacobs, Alicia Rodriquez, Janet Freitag, and Ann Dodson.

My family stands at the center of my work and my life. I am profoundly grateful for the four generations that I am privileged to call "mine." Their presence is a constant reminder of what really matters.

The book is dedicated to two people. As a young woman, my mother aspired to a career full of challenge and achievement. She found another "career," as a wife and mother. She did not live to see the book completed, but I hope she would have seen something of herself in the women whose lives appear in these pages. My husband, Larry Lynch, read every page at least three times, woke up early and stayed up late listening to my arguments, and offered advice – not always solicited or appreciated – at the drop of a hat. I am ninety percent sure the book would not have been possible without him.

Twenty-two years ago, I got a bear by the tail and couldn't let go. Newspapering has become my life, and I fear I'd be miserably unhappy if, while I'm in my prime years, I should forgo, or be crowded out, of my calling. . . . I'd be daffy if I thought I'd be content away from the newspaper profession. – Agness Underwood, *Newspaperwoman*

When Agness Underwood penned this paragraph in 1949, she was forty-seven years old and the city editor of the *Los Angeles Herald and Express*. In her ambition to be a journalist Underwood joined more than 23,000 other women who went to work as editors and reporters between 1920 and 1950. During that time women in the journalistic workforce grew from 16.8 percent to 32 percent.[1] And at a time when less than 20 percent of married women in America worked, nearly 40 percent of women journalists combined careers and marriage.[2] All of the women sought professional success, a sense of accomplishment, and a feeling of connectedness, both to the larger world and to a community of accomplished colleagues.

Most female journalists worked for women's pages published in newspapers and magazines. But a few hundred won coveted jobs as front-page reporters, working alongside male colleagues on city desks and in courthouses, police stations, city halls, foreign capitals, and, finally, on World War II battlefields. These women knew they were fortunate, that they had succeeded through a combination of tenacity, pluck, courage, and the willingness to work endless hours while often earning far less money than men.

They were also at the right place at the right time. Since women first began knocking on newsroom doors in the years after the Civil War, men vociferously and publicly opposed their entrance into the profession, declaring them unsuitable to this most masculine of jobs. They might toil in feature sections, writing about recipes, social gatherings, and children, but women were temperamentally unsuited to work in newsrooms, where the pace was like lightning and men smoked, drank, and swore. Or so the argument went. Before World War I only a handful of truly exceptional women crossed the gender barrier dividing "soft" and "hard" news.

But in the years following World War I, as many historians have noted, old ideas and practices began to seem outmoded. Women capitalized on shifts in the cultural winds – the achievement of suffrage, a developing youth culture, a focus on modernity – to move in new directions during the 1920s. It was a decade that the historian Nancy Woloch has described as "a crossroads at which different themes of women's history overlapped and entwined."[3]

Female journalists of Agness Underwood's generation knew enough to pay homage to the few courageous women who came before. Elizabeth Cochrane ("Nellie Bly") exposed corruption, unearthed scandal, and performed "stunts" for Joseph Pulitzer's *New York World*. Marie Manning wrote stories and advice columns for Pulitzer. Winifred Black ("Annie Laurie") wrote for William Randolph Hearst in San Francisco and New York. Peggy Hull worked for several papers and covered the Russian Civil War as the first American woman credentialed as a war correspondent. African American women journalists had their own heroes, most notably the fearless Ida B. Wells-Barnett, who crusaded against lynching and racism.

But it was Underwood's generation of female journalists who pried open the newsroom doors for good, paving the way for women's acceptance in the world of front-page journalism. Hers was the generation that proved women were not too sensitive or emotional to work alongside hard-boiled men in this high-stress environment. From the 1920s through the 1940s, women "manned" city desks, covered political debates in Washington DC, tangled with officers in police stations, and documented human misery resulting from racism and the Depression. They interviewed world leaders, slept in huts, and trudged through mud in war zones. By the end of the 1940s few professional obstacles remained. Women could not break the gender barrier of the all-male press clubs, their salaries were often half those of their male counterparts, and they were not hired nearly as frequently as men. But for the post–World War II generation of women, front-page reporting had become an attainable career choice.

Underwood's generation did more than open the door for other female journalists, however. The public examples they provided helped to reshape larger cultural ideas about gender. Ultimately their accomplishments helped to illuminate what a later generation of women would call the "social construction of gender," for it became harder to justify deeply held notions of inherent male and female traits when women succeeded at doing the same work as men.

In some respects front-page women can be compared to pioneers in other professions, such as the female social scientists, who fought their way into graduate schools early in the twentieth century. Rosalind Rosenberg has detailed how these women used themselves as examples and used their research to suggest new possibilities for looking at the relationship between biology and gender.[4] None of these researchers won lasting fame, according to Rosenberg, but their studies "formulated theories about intelligence, personality development, and sex roles that not only altered American thinking about the nature of women and men, but also affected the whole course of American social science."[5]

On the surface, the ivied walls of academe and litter-strewn newsrooms would seem to have little in common. But the men who worked in both milieus shared a mind-set and a gender-coded language that served to keep women out of their fraternity. Joan Scott has argued that this "coded" language long enabled men to set the terms of debate in professional fields. Women who challenged these codes risked being viewed as disputing nature. To breach the fortress walls of the research laboratory and the newsroom, women had to do more than knock insistently at the door. They had to learn to use the male language to turn gendered ideas back on themselves.[6]

Front-page women, like their sisters in science, succeeded in this endeavor by openly acknowledging gender stereotypes, then laboring to expose the faulty logic behind them through personal example and by learning to speak the same language as their male peers. But front-page women operated on a larger, public stage not readily available to female pioneers in science. They could capitalize on their access to a mass audience that, in some sense, "saw" women working behind their bylines.[7]

Like the scientists Rosenberg studied, most front-page reporters never gained fame, acclaim, or even much prominence outside their chosen profession. While some outstanding reporters became celebrities, most were less well-known than other famous women who began to appear in such fields as aviation, athletics, and film after World War I. But women in non-journalistic careers relied on other people to keep them in the public eye – movie studios, press agents, and reporters, including front-page women who avidly wrote about their exploits. More than women in any other profession at this time, female front-page reporters had the power to shape cultural perceptions, through their bylines, via interviews they gave in magazines, advice they offered in career books, and in the stories they chose to cover.

This study examines ways in which front-page women succeeded in gaining acceptance and respect from male colleagues as they helped pave the way for new ideas about gender and society. Their accomplishment depended on a clever, unacknowledged, and probably unconscious strategy: refusing to confront openly longstanding prejudices about women and ingrained cultural ideas about women's inherent qualities while laboring intensely to demonstrate to a larger audience that these stereotypes were inaccurate and unfair.

Through much of this period women labored to defuse male antagonism by demonstrating an almost obsessive toughness and hyper-dependability. To counteract male concerns that this "masculine" profession might make them too much like men, front-page women were careful to reveal some of their more feminine attributes as well; for example, they baked cookies and sewed on buttons for colleagues, dressed nicely, and flattered male egos. Reading between the lines in their stories, in statements about themselves, and in advice they offered, it is possible to see these women subtly and cleverly taking on gender stereotypes. They suggested, for example, that while some men denigrated women's abilities to withstand newsroom pressures, the men they knew personally knew better than to make blanket generalizations. Some suggested that only exceptional women could succeed in front-page journalism, both reinforcing the stereotypes and opening the newsroom door for other "exceptional" women. The few women who held positions of authority in journalism mentored other women.

The unwillingness of female front-page journalists to confront larger gender stereotypes might lead some to argue against their importance in reshaping cultural views of women's roles. I would strongly disagree with this argument. These women had no framework for challenging gender ideology as culturally constructed, since that concept did not exist until much later. If such a notion had existed, front-page women still would not have directly challenged larger cultural assumptions because doing so only would have hindered their progress and that of other women. Specifically, it would distance them psychologically from an audience not prepared for a frontal assault on longstanding and deeply felt ideas about who women and men were. Pioneering female journalists needed the support of this audience to keep their own jobs and to increase opportunities for other women. By putting themselves on a public stage, then acting out a new set of gender roles, front-page women led their audience to begin seeing women in a new light without knowing they were being led in this direction.

It is possible to track the success of their strategy through changes in the ways they presented themselves publicly. By the 1940s many women journalists were less willing to acquiesce to stereotypes and less cautious about their role in the newsroom. Popular culture makes it possible to see the impact they had on a mass audience as well. Magazines began tracking the women's progress in the 1920s, and by the 1930s dozens of films had front-page reporters as protagonists. Women journalists were even the subject of a doctoral dissertation from Columbia University in 1935, and by the 1940s a popular comic strip, "Brenda Starr," featured a glamorized version of the exploits of a female front-page reporter. Further evidence exists in the thousands of women who began to see journalism as a viable career choice between 1920 and 1950, when the number of females in the profession quadrupled.

Cultural venues reflected many of the challenges faced by women who chose this non-traditional career but suggested that all of their experiences were similar. This was not the case. Each woman experienced a unique set of circumstances depending on the kind of publication she worked for, the audience she wrote for, and the kind of reporting she chose to do. Films and other forms of mainstream popular culture focused on the experiences of white, middle-class women and ignored the important contributions of African American women to the field of journalism and to changing perceptions of women.

Looking at white women alone provides only part of the story of how front-page journalists reshaped larger cultural attitudes. African American women played a significant role in this effort as well, and I believe that examining their experiences alongside those of white women brings an additional dimension to understanding the pervasiveness of gender ideology and the myriad ways in which women worked to counteract it. Racial issues that necessitated a strong and united community to confront oppression shaped the lives of black women. Many black women found opportunities in journalism because the black press represented such a crucial component of this community. But many black men held the same attitudes as white men about women's inherent qualities and preferred gender roles. As a result, black women also experienced skepticism and lack of acceptance in male journalism circles. This lack of acceptance required black women to adopt strategies similar in some ways to those of white women.

African American and white women found a sense of personal fulfillment and purpose in journalism; both viewed themselves as pioneers and role models for other women. Women from both groups had to negotiate the alien territory of front-page journalism on their own. And women of both ethnic groups found a community in journalism, although these communities differed.

Black women journalists used the connections between

the black press and other social and political institutions to expand their own personal boundaries and to suggest how, as shapers of cultural images, they might elevate the status of the community as well.[8] White women journalists had no such built-in community. In some ways, white women benefited from this lack of cohesion because it allowed them to succeed as individuals and to downplay any suggestion that they aimed to advance an agenda that would lift all female boats along with their own. In other ways, however, this lack of community enhanced their sense of isolation. Some white front-page women joined women's press clubs, yet this offered only a tenuous community. The only thing white women journalists had in common was being disparaged, at some point, by men.

This study is divided into four chapters. The first chapter tracks women's movement into front-page journalism, and it examines their experiences through their own words and their portrayals in popular culture venues including magazines, books, and films. I have chosen to look only at women working on large metropolitan newspapers because they reached the widest audience. Thousands of other women worked as front-page reporters in suburban newspapers throughout the country and, clearly, they also played an important role in enlarging women's sphere in the field of journalism. But women working at big city papers got most of the attention from mass media outlets, which held more power to shape cultural perceptions and ideas in society as a whole.

For this same reason I chose to examine only mainstream newspapers. Alternative or specialty publications tended to have a limited focus, for example on politics or business. I recognize that this approach excludes the contributions of women such as Dorothy Day of *The Catholic Worker* and Josephine Herbst and Anna Louise Strong, both of whom worked as foreign correspondents. But all three women wrote for politically oriented publications with a leftist bent, and this precluded their appeal to a mass, mostly middle-class, audience. I also recognize that the term "mainstream" differs in the white and black communities. Because of finances, black urban publications tended to be weekly, while white metropolitan papers were published daily. Black papers also had lower circulations – primarily because of the limited finances of their readers – and a single paper was often passed from reader to reader. But the importance of black newspapers for the community makes them comparable in influence to newspapers of the time serving a larger white audience.

Each of the succeeding three chapters focuses on a single woman who had a unique experience as a front-page journalist. Ruth Finney worked for Scripps Howard News Alliance as one of the premier political reporters in Washington DC. Charlotta Bass edited and wrote for the *California Eagle*, a Los Angeles–based African American newspaper that played a key role in the local black community. Agness Underwood covered sensational crimes and Hollywood for the *Los Angeles Evening Herald and Express* before becoming city editor in 1947. I selected these particular women because they held high-level jobs, had enough of a sense of self to write of their thoughts and experiences in autobiographies, and clearly had a sense that what they achieved would have some effect on other women. Additionally, all three women were respected by their colleagues, both male and female, and all won honors within their communities and profession. Finney was the first woman nominated for a Pulitzer Prize, for reporting on the power industry, in 1931. Bass was the first African American in Los Angeles chosen to serve on a county Grand Jury, and she trained a generation of black journalists in that city. In 1947 Underwood became the first woman city editor at a major American newspaper. When she retired, entertainer Bob Hope emceed the standing-room-only festivities.

All three women began their careers in California, and two of them spent their entire careers in the state. Front-page journalism was a professional frontier for women throughout the country during this time, and many significant women worked in the West – a geographical frontier as well. This region of the country was significant in the development of journalism overall as well as in the experiences of individual women. Several of the country's most prominent publishers began their professional lives west of the Appalachians. They include *New York Times* publisher Adolph Ochs, who started out in Tennessee; Joseph Patterson, who published the *Chicago Tribune*; Joseph Pulitzer, who revolutionized journalism as publisher of the *St. Louis Post-Dispatch* before moving on to New York and the *World*; and William Randolph Hearst, who cut his journalistic teeth on the *San Francisco Examiner* before taking his sensational brand of newspapering to New York and then to the rest of the country.

The frontier has long been viewed as offering many opportunities for ambitious young men. And as many historians have noted, the West also offered women the freedom to explore new roles and professions, including journalism. In the nineteenth century the frontier was dotted with towns, and most towns were served by their own newspapers, run by families, by husbands and wives, or in some cases, by women alone.[9]

California, the ultimate frontier for adventurers in the nineteenth century, became the final destination for people of all ethnic backgrounds by the 1920s. The benign climate and business-friendly environment lured thousands of white residents to Los Angeles. Its burgeoning film industry brought the city renown and notoriety. African Americans came west to escape the longstanding oppression they suffered in other regions of the country.

A wide variety of newspapers documented the development of industry, the struggle over water and power, racial

conflicts, and scandal-plagued lives of celebrities. The intersection of race and politics provided opportunity for a few
black women to document the African American experience
and to fight for racial justice. The connection among politics,
culture, and media made California a good place for ambitious white women to earn nationwide prominence as
front-page reporters. California's status as the world's film
capital gave them wider exposure as well. When producers
and directors looked for interesting stories and characters,
women reporters in California provided both the inspiration and the story material. The resulting films, such as *His
Girl Friday*, depicted women, striding clearly and purpose-
fully, through male terrain.

Like the vast majority of women in other professions,
few front-page women journalists during this period, black
or white, risked labeling themselves feminists. And yet
their actions can be viewed in retrospect as protofeminist.
The careful way they worked and lived, so as not to discredit
their gender, offered an important first step for later generations of women who would publicly declare themselves
feminists and who would debate myriad ways in which
gender stereotypes are socially constructed. The attitudes
and behavior of front-page women might seem to presage
the kind of feminism some scholars have called "liberal" or
"equal rights" feminism: reflecting a belief in gender equality and the Enlightenment emphasis on individual rights
and responsibilities rather than the essentialist or social
brand of feminism that embraced women as members of a
larger group with common concerns and needs.[10]

To categorize women in this way understates the com-
plexity of their lives and work, for they had a foot in both
camps. Women journalists, black and white, understood at
some level that gender discrimination affected all women,
and that this experience forged some sort of common bond
among them, however tenuous. And they believed that they

could prove instrumental in fostering larger social changes. But they also believed in individual careers, individual strategies for advancement, and saw themselves, individually, as the equals of men. If, as individuals, they did not advance the cause of feminism, their attitudes and behaviors at least hinted at possibilities for the future.

Front-Page Women Journalists, 1920-1950

1. Crossing the Threshold

Women in Front-Page Journalism

No excuses are accepted. If one doesn't know how to do the assignment given, one finds out – in a hurry. One succeeds today, tomorrow and the day after that, or finds another way of earning a living. The wise reporter is never without a toothbrush or a comb, for assignments sometimes do not end with the setting sun and sometimes they lead far afield. – Ruth Finney, "The Reporter"

Ruth Finney, a Washington DC correspondent for Scripps Howard News Alliance, offered her observations in an essay aimed at young women seeking careers in front-page journalism for a 1934 book. A veteran of sixteen years in the profession at the time of her writing, her appraisal does not seem designed to encourage readers to rush right out to their local newspapers and apply for jobs. Without hitting anyone over the head with a typewriter, Finney suggested that the field was not for the faint of heart, for those who lacked stamina, or for those whose feelings were easily hurt. In short, front-page journalism was not for anyone but the exceptional person. She never mentioned the word "woman," but her words seem designed to illustrate the "maleness" of a reporter's job. Practitioners should show up with combs and toothbrushes, for example, but not with lipstick or face powder.

It is impossible, nearly seventy years after the book's publication, to know Finney's motives for this cautionary approach. Was she trying to discourage female competition? Was she trying to save women who might simply be looking for excitement the bother of rejection or disappointment?

Was she touting qualities in herself that allowed her to succeed in such a male enterprise? Her remarks did make one thing clear: front-page journalism was fun and rewarding for those who managed to make a successful career out of it. "Life is lived in the center of things," she wrote. "The reporter goes everywhere . . . surveys the world while others see only a part."[1]

Finney was not the only woman front-page journalist who seemed to be picking her way through a minefield in appraising her job. Three years earlier, in another advice book for aspiring women journalists, Emma Bugbee, a reporter at the *New York Herald-Tribune* and president of the New York Newspaper Women's Club, acknowledged that a "romantic glamour surrounds our girl reporter. The allure is second only to films." Why? Because reporters "come into contact with exhilarating, interesting people." But Bugbee, like Finney, was quick to warn readers that success required industry, tenacity, and "deference while bending people to one's will." Potential drawbacks included "strain on nerves . . . loneliness, meals in strange restaurants."[2]

A partial explanation for the careful words of Finney and Bugbee may lie in yet another book about journalism, also published in 1934. This one, however, was written by a man, Stanley Walker, city editor at the *New York Herald-Tribune*. He described life in the maelstrom of a metropolitan daily newsroom. One chapter, titled "A Gallery of Angels," made it clear from the male perspective that women were not welcome in the inner sanctum. Walker reeled off a list of perceived female personality traits that excluded them from the newspaper fraternity. According to popular lore, women "sulk at reproof and if criticized, burst into tears. They say no to sex in business, but seduce the copyreader with a wife and three children. They depend on men to help them in tough spots, then double cross them. They possess no sense of humor. They claim reliability, then quit for marriage." Walker assured his women readers, however, that he did not agree with these sentiments.[3]

Women front-page reporters might argue that this stereotype was inaccurate, not to mention demeaning. But mere words alone would not help them get a foot in the door or gain permanent residency in the newsroom. For that they had to set out to personally contradict each and every aspect of the stereotype. They had to take criticism without flinching or crying. They could never ask for help. They had to take the job seriously but still possess a sense of humor. In other words, they had to demonstrate stereotypical male qualities, or at least the qualities that men liked to think they possessed.

But did male reporters actually possess those traits? Not according to Walker, who acknowledged as much in a 1931 magazine article he wrote for the *American Mercury*, describing the city editor's job. "He is like the manager of a baseball team. . . . Each has to contend with sulkiness, genius, jealousy, money and overeating. Each knows the disappointment of seeing a presumably good man fall down on a job."[4] City editors themselves occasionally fell short of perfection, according to Walker. "They are mean and generous, cruel and kind, yes-men and snarlers, indolent and dynamic, roughnecks and urbane gentlemen, lushers and Puritans."[5]

Seen in this context, the careful way Finney and Bugbee approached the topic of women in journalism suggests the possibility of a purposeful strategy, one based in real-life experience. It's possible that by discouraging all but the women best suited to the job, Finney, Bugbee, and many other female front-page journalists who wrote and talked about their work in the period between 1920 and the end of World War II, increased the probability that those entering the field would have the personality traits necessary to succeed. And each woman who succeeded paved the way for others. On the other hand, encouraging all women to enter the field would only mean certain failure for some who might exhibit stereotypical female failings or who might quit in exasperation. This failure would perpetuate the long-standing antifemale bias.

From this vantage point Finney and Bugbee clearly saw themselves as gatekeepers as well as trailblazers. How could they not? It had become clear by the 1930s that the public at large had taken notice of their work. How else does one account for the films featuring front-page women as main characters and the proliferation of books and magazine articles by and about them? In addition, these women understood the importance of what they were doing. At a time when women's autobiographies were not commonplace, many female journalists wrote them, and a number of them were published.

The most significant evidence attesting to growing public awareness of front-page women lies in figures from the U.S. decennial census. The numbers show thousands of women entering the profession, despite discouragement from men and a less than enthusiastic endorsement from the women practitioners themselves. In the 1920 census, 5,730 women were listed as journalists.[6] By the 1930s, the numbers had doubled, and they continued to grow rapidly throughout the interwar period. By the 1950 census, nearly 30,000 women called themselves journalists, and they represented 32 percent of the profession.[7]

The majority of women entering the field during this period worked on smaller newspapers, on larger papers covering the so-called "soft side" women's pages, or as staff writers and freelancers on magazines. It is not possible to determine the number of women working as front-page, or "hard-news" reporters, who had desks in the newsroom and worked alongside men covering politics, crime, economic policy, and war. It is clear from reading autobiographies, biographies, congressional directories, and a doctoral dissertation from Columbia University that the number of female hard-news reporters also grew significantly during this period, although they remained a distinct minority.

Women in every region of the country went to work for all kinds of newspapers: tabloids, wire services such as the Associated Press and United Press, newspaper chains such as Scripps Howard, and papers owned by individuals. Prominent front-page women tended to cluster at larger papers in big cities, such as New York, Washington DC, San Francisco, and Los Angeles. In big cities, papers competed fiercely for readers, and women writers bolstered circulation. Although most publishers and editors discouraged women, a few, including William Randolph Hearst with a publishing empire centered in New York and California, openly encouraged them.

In her 1935 Columbia University dissertation, doctoral candidate Iona Robertson Logie included nine front-page women working in New York.[8] In *Ladies of the Press*, a 1936 book documenting the progress of women in journalism, Ishbel Ross discussed nearly a dozen top-rated front-page reporters, including Ruth Finney.[9] And the congressional directory, which tallied reporters credentialed to cover Congress, cited thirty-two women reporters in 1942, up from eight in 1924.[10] A year later *Newsweek* magazine estimated the number of accredited female Capitol correspondents at seventy-four.[11]

Virtually all of the studies, articles, and books about female journalists published during the 1920s–1940s focused on white women. African American women journalists, as in other fields, were mostly invisible to white popular culture and white media in general. With few exceptions white newspapers ignored the African American community, except to reinforce negative stereotypes about crime, poverty, and racial incidents. But black women found opportunities to move into front-page reporting as well. African

American women and men worked almost exclusively on black-owned papers during this period. But there were a few exceptions. One woman who did cross the journalistic racial divide was Delilah Beasley, who covered the African American community for the white-owned *Tribune* in Oakland, California, and who also published a book about black pioneers in California.[12]

African American papers were, unarguably, more focused on politics, especially as they related to discrimination and oppression, than white papers. Like white papers, however, they covered every aspect of their communities. Since many reporters on black newspapers covered the spectrum from soft news to hard news it is possible to argue that most African American female journalists were front-page reporters.

While advice and other books focused on journalism ignore African American women altogether, it is clear from reading their own accounts that they labored under many of the same stereotypes experienced by white women.[13] Ellen Tarry, who came to New York in the 1920s and tried to get a job at an African American newspaper, reported being treated in a condescending, patronizing manner by an editor who claimed that "most newspaperwomen were ugly and he didn't think I was the type."[14] Marvel Cooke, who also entered the profession of journalism in the 1920s, was initially hired by the *Amsterdam News* in New York as a society editor and had to work her way into hard news. In the newsroom, Cooke recalled in an interview, she was treated differently than male reporters.[15] And Charlotta Bass, who became a prominent figure in African American journalism, recalled that when she started in the profession, before World War I, black male leaders in Los Angeles were skeptical of the new "girl" publisher of the *California Eagle*. Bass was well into her thirties at the time.[16]

Despite all of the pitfalls and frustrations, for African American and white female journalists, front-page reporting seemed worth the struggle and undoubtedly was more rewarding to women at this time than other, more readily available, jobs: semi-skilled operator in manufacturing, stenography, teaching, bookkeeping, and switchboard operator for white women, and domestic work for black women.[17] Front-page journalism offered them a front-row seat to history and the opportunity to shape history, for themselves and for others of their sex. Opening newsroom doors for themselves and the careful way they presented themselves to the public – composed of both their male colleagues and a mass audience of readers – enabled front-page women to participate in the ongoing public dialogue about gender, specifically about whether inherent female traits should prevent women from following their dreams. And their examples, like those of other pioneers, helped to change the terms of debate on gender. "It's hard to explain the fascination of newspaper work," wrote Mary Margaret McBride, a 1920s reporter who later became a noted radio talk show host and a woman who clearly understood the power of gender stereotypes and language. "Once you've had it, no matter where you go or what you do, no matter how much money you make or how famous you become, your proudest boast is that you were once a newspaperman."[18]

Opening the Door

As many historians of journalism have noted, women started seriously knocking on newsroom doors in the years after the Civil War when massive industrialization, urbanization, and immigration fueled the explosion of newspapers and magazines and fostered a journalism largely oriented toward sensationalism and political and social reform.[19] By 1900 there were nearly 2,000 English-language papers in the United States, and some big city papers enjoyed circulations of a half-million.[20] But only a few truly exceptional women had managed to gain a toehold in front-page journalism to this point.

Although they wanted to be taken seriously, white women journalists in the latter decades of the nineteenth century and first decade or so of the twentieth century had to acquiesce to stereotypes depicting them as emotional and entertaining in order to succeed. Hired to write stories that would wring tears of sorrow and sympathy from readers, female reporters thus earned the sobriquet "sob sisters." Pre–World War I women also proved more than willing to perform "stunts," sometimes dangerous activities designed to amuse and astound readers.

Female prewar journalists often allowed themselves to be used as objects by allowing public attention to be drawn to their more traditional sides so as not to frighten male editors and audience members. Thus Elizabeth Cochrane ("Nellie Bly") emphasized her own attractiveness, even as she sped around the world faster than anyone had done before in seventy-two days in late 1889 and early 1890 for the *New York World*. Marie Manning ("Beatrice Fairfax") emphasized her helpfulness as an advice columnist for William Randolph Hearst and Joseph Pulitzer. And Peggy Hull, who briefly covered World War I as an unaccredited reporter for a Cleveland newspaper, acted as a personal shopper to hometown boys stationed in France, while writing human interest stories about French lifestyles and families.[21] Virtually no white female front-page journalists combined marriage and career at this time. Marriage meant the end of their career for all but a few.

Post–World War I women reporters combined marriage and career, and they publicly decried the willingness of the older generation to allow themselves to be used as objects of amusement and entertainment. Florence Finch Kelly, writing in 1939, reflected the disdainful postwar view of women stunters and sob sisters. Looking back, Kelly surmised that editors of the prewar period, who might have been willing to hire more women "were revolted by the spectacle of these stunting, shrieking and sobbing young women … and their attitude toward women wanting newspaper employment … stiffened into antagonism."[22] Yet another career book for women published in the 1930s also disdained this approach as "waxing sloppily sentimental over everything from a lost dog to a hardened criminal," declaring it "passe."[23] Some postwar front-page women reporters went even further in trying to dislodge women from the sob sister niche. Agness Underwood, a Los Angeles crime reporter and city editor, turned the stereotype on its head by suggesting that some male reporters could "bring out the feminine point of view with skill superior to many female reporters."[24]

Postwar African American women did not have to go quite as far to distance themselves from the tactics of prewar black pioneers. Their primary role model was Ida B. Wells, who made a career crusading against lynching and racial discrimination in newspapers, pamphlets, and books. She presented herself as serious and uncompromising at all times. But Wells still had to overcome prejudices of black men who, like white men, jealously guarded their prerogatives. For example, in the early 1900s Wells helped found the National Association for the Advancement of Colored People but was denied a leadership role because she was viewed as strident.[25] In her autobiography Wells quoted T. Thomas Fortune, publisher of the *New York Age*, if she "were a man she would be a humming independent in politics. She has plenty of nerve and is as sharp as a steel trap."[26]

If postwar women succeeded in putting distance between themselves and their sob sister predecessors, timing was the primary catalyst. Many Americans in the decades after the war embraced modernity and distanced themselves from longstanding traditions and ideas. The war propelled America, albeit reluctantly, into the larger world community and fostered a more sophisticated approach to politics and economics. At the same time, politicians, businessmen, and advertisers promoted a consumer mentality in which being "modern" meant buying things and focusing on the image of success. This proved a boon for advertisers, who relentlessly promoted modernity in pursuit of sales and who subsidized most forms of media. Meanwhile the advent of radio and talking pictures – also dependent on advertising – fueled a national culture based on celebrity, youth, a more open sexuality, and image.[27] These political and social trends propelled some women into the public eye with glamorous new careers such as aviation, athletics, film, evangelism, and front-page reporting.

The achievement of suffrage in 1920 fueled new debates about the nature of equality in arenas larger than the strictly political; this included wage work for women. According to Alice Kessler-Harris, "independent wage earning seemed the logical next step, an intrinsic part of the feminist agenda."[28] Divisions among women themselves ultimately doomed this agenda, but some exceptional women were able to use the enlarged sphere of debate to sell themselves to male employers who had long subscribed to the belief in individualism – for themselves at least. Susan Ware examined this postsuffrage mentality through the lens of aviator Amelia Earhart. Ware argued that exceptional women could use individual talents during the 1920s and 1930s to transcend stereotypical notions of gender. But Earhart's strategy mirrored that of front-page women by offering the public her personal example of independence and ambition, rather than publicly challenging or debating the stereotypes.[29] Ware saw Earhart's strategy at work in the lives of notable women in other fields during this time as well, including actor Katharine Hepburn and front-page journalist Dorothy Thompson. This individualist approach also was evident in the pages of *Independent Woman*, a magazine started in the 1920s that focused on the accomplishments of exceptional woman, including many journalists, who also wrote articles for the magazine.

The media gave exceptional women in all fields a public stage on which to act out modern gender roles and identities for a mass audience avidly interested in their exploits. Because journalism is an enterprise that promotes independence, it offered ambitious women the opportunity to forge their own careers and to offer a silent rebuttal to traditional notions about gender. But postwar changes in the field of journalism itself brought enhanced opportunities for women. "It is only since the World War," wrote Florence Finch Kelly, "that they have been able to go steadily on, with opportunities increasing, their own numbers growing rapidly."[30]

The profound changes in journalism that occurred at this time can largely be attributed to the burgeoning consumer culture and to an enhanced interest in political developments in other parts of the world. Both of these forces fostered intense competition between newspapers and other forms of media, and among newspapers themselves, all of which vied for scarce advertising dollars. During the 1920s the exploding popularity of radio compelled mainstream media to introduce interpretive magazines and photo-driven tabloid newspapers; the former sought to siphon off some of the "sophisticated" audience, while the latter aimed to entice readers at the other end of the spectrum, those enamored of scandals and sensation.

The consumer revolution fed by advertising created a seemingly insatiable demand for news in the 1920s. Daily newspaper circulation climbed from 22.4 million copies a day in 1910 to 39.6 million in 1930. And newspaper advertising revenue tripled between 1915 and 1924, growing from $275 million to $800 million annually.[31] But publishers and editors had to think creatively to gain a larger market share of this revenue. The fact that some did not can be seen from the shrinking number of newspapers themselves – from 2,200 English-language papers in 1910 to 1,942 in 1930. Some of this decline can be attributed to mergers, but many papers folded because they could not withstand the competition.[32]

To sell papers, mainstream publishers and editors began to experiment with different approaches, ranging from an increased focus on human interest stories that included sensation and scandal and celebrities, to an effort to sell themselves and their papers as fair, impartial, and objective in presenting the news. Sociologist Michael Schudson saw the trend toward objectivity as a result of the climate of skepticism that arose in the aftermath of the World War I propaganda campaign. He also saw it amid the growing reliance on public relations as a way to sell businesses to the public.[33] Schudson argued that these developments led to the wider recognition that emotion, rather than reason, governed the world. This enabled publishers and editors to promote themselves as interpreters of reality for their audiences. Whatever the catalyst, by selling themselves as purveyors of objectivity, publishers encouraged their readers to see them as more serious and accurate than their colorful counterparts, an important selling point in a highly competitive market.

Both of these approaches indirectly aided aspiring women journalists. The human interest emphasis enabled them to capitalize on the longstanding notion that women could write this type of story better than men, and the goal of objectivity allowed them to argue that newspaper managers should use objective and fair criteria in hiring new reporters as well as in publishing stories. Among those who capitalized on these shifts in the winds were a trio of women who worked for the wire services: Ruth Cowan, Lorena Hickok, and Bess Furman. Others included Ruth Finney, who worked in Washington DC; Genevieve Forbes Herrick, who worked in Chicago; and Agness Underwood, who worked in Los Angeles.

Foreign reporting also provided women new opportunities. Although America professed to be an isolationist country after World War I, mainstream newspapers joined new interpretive publications such as *Time* and *The New Yorker* in covering the world outside the United States in the 1920s.[34] According to historian Morrell Heald, the world war "turned international journalism from a casual, amateur affair to serious business."[35] Because foreign reporting was a new field, it had no established rules and no reporting staffs already in place. Therefore, enterprising women could hire onto large papers, initially as freelance writers and then work their way up to staff writers. By demonstrating their journalistic and interpersonal skills, a few managed to attain star status. Dorothy Thompson and Anne O'Hare McCormick were two women who took advantage of this new world stage during the 1920s as they gained prominence as foreign correspondents for the *Philadelphia Public Ledger* and the *New York Times*, respectively.

African American newspapers never competed with mainstream white papers, or with radio, for advertising dollars, but they too reflected post–World War I changes in media and in the black community itself that made newspapers seem an essential purchase rather than a luxury. Black newspapers capitalized specifically on the flight of blacks from the South to northern cities, creating a strong demand for a "community conscious press" focused on "'the minutiae of Black life' – social events no other publishers would cover and appreciate."[36] African American newspapers also began to reflect the more assertive attitudes their community adopted in the post–World War I era, as veterans who had fought to keep the world "safe for democracy" came home to find democracy still sadly lacking for themselves. Most publishers of black papers were men, including Robert S. Abbott of the *Chicago Defender* and William Monroe Trotter of the *Boston Guardian*. But the powerful role traditionally played by black women in the community afforded them new journalistic opportunities. In the postwar era several newspapers were published by black women: Mary Ellen Vaughan founded the *Murfeesboro Union* in Alabama in the 1920s, Thelma Childs Taylor published the *Topeka Plaindealer* in Kansas, and Charlotta Bass published the *California Eagle* with her husband, Joseph, in Los Angeles. All aimed to make their newspapers the instruments of social uplift and harsh critics of American apartheid.[37]

Both black and white women capitalized on timing to gain access to the newsroom. Most importantly, perhaps, they capitalized on the sense of possibility in the postwar world. To turn this possibility into a true gain, however, they had to carefully navigate through rugged male terrain, present themselves as unique and highly adaptable individuals, offer unspoken testimony to the possibilities of larger social change.

The Newsroom: Inviolate Male Space

Getting through the door was a first step, but it represented a gigantic leap for women, according to those who had tried and mostly failed to gain a toehold earlier. Advice columnist Marie Manning described how zealously men guarded the newsroom door in the pre-World War I period. Women were sometimes "summoned to the city room for assignments," she wrote, but none had desks in "that inviolate masculine stronghold."[38] Rheta Childe Dorr, a contemporary of Manning's, bemoaned the fact that, in the first decade of the twentieth century, "as far as I could see I lived in a world entirely hostile to women," where "every man's hand was held out to help young fellows beginning in life. The brightest woman waited in the chicken coop."[39]

In fact, everything about the physical layout and ambiance of the newsroom fairly shouted the words "Men Only." On every newspaper, the large, open spaces variously called the "city room" and the "newsroom," were cluttered, noisy, and filthy. Disheveled reporters sat at battered desks loaded down with piles of paper, pencils, ashtrays, food debris, and the more than occasional bottle of liquor. Two separate T-shaped clusters of desks pushed together comprised the city desk and the copy desk. At the former, shirt-sleeved and frequently ill-tempered city editors ruled over this seemingly chaotic space. They barked out assignments, yelled for copy, laid out pages, and answered incessantly ringing phones. The city editor, noted one reporter, "receives all the letters of protest, listens to tirades from angry persons . . . placates them, reasons with them and continues to print his paper."[40] At the copy desk, where the editing took place, profane, cigar-smoking men wrote headlines and tried to make stories fit the space allotted. Piles of paper also littered the floor, where they shared space with discarded food and ashes from cigarettes, cigars, and pipes. The smell of ever-present smoke clung to clothing and furniture and cast a smoglike pall over the entire newsroom.

The pace was breathtaking. Daily newspapers often had up to six deadlines beginning early in the morning and extending late into the night. Bigger papers had day and night shifts. Weekly newspapers enjoyed a somewhat more leisurely pace, but news could break at the last minute there as well. Reporters never knew when they would be called out on breaking stories or whether the news would require an all-night vigil at a police station, a visit to a gory crime scene, or a somnambulant few hours spent in a town council meeting room. Back in the newsroom stories frequently had to be written at the speed of a courtroom typist or dictated from the nearest pay phone out in the field. Shouts of "Where's my rewrite man?" could be heard a dozen times a day. Courtesy, deference, and patience were not part of the newsman's resume, or vocabulary.

The language used to describe journalistic functions and newsroom equipment also had a distinctly masculine cast.

When reporters wrote their stories, they "slugged" them, which meant putting a word identifying the story at the top of each typewritten page. The word presumably derives from the slugs of type used in linotype machines. More than one neophyte female reporter was rattled at the first use of the term. Joan Lowell, who spent a year on a Boston tabloid in the early 1930s, nearly jumped out of her chair when the city editor told the copy desk to "slug Joan Lowell," she recalled. The copy editor's reply, "Why doesn't she slug herself?"[41] Early morning editions were called "bulldogs," and reporters and editors sat in an area of the newsroom called the "bullpen." When editors wanted to denote the death of a story, they "spiked" it by impaling it on a vertical nail attached to a board. And the newsroom library, containing copies of old stories and old photographs, was called "the morgue."

Women, armed with ambition and the desire to cover hard news in the 1920s had to navigate this male terrain like a high-wire act. They had to live amid the clutter, profanity, and rudeness without complaint, compete with men on stories, but not boast about besting them. And they had to demonstrate just enough "female" traits – kindness, compassion, thoughtfulness – to suggest their presence would brighten up the workplace. Above all, they could never suggest that all women were capable of handling this most difficult job.

Some women could not handle the strain. Journalist Catharine Brody, in a 1926 magazine article for the *American Mercury*, declared herself sad that "God made me, not in his image, but as a woman. I do not know where this fact can assume more tragic significance than on the mourners' bench outside a city room. Inside his shop, the most hard-boiled newspaper man is still a knight in shining armor, self-appointed to save lovely woman from the perils of the news assignment."[42]

But a growing number of women did take on the challenges and thrived through quiet determination. Agness Underwood, who began her career in 1923, willingly sewed buttons on the jackets of her male colleagues at the *Los Angeles Record* while scooping them on stories. Charlotta Bass publicly deferred to her husband and co-publisher Joseph Bass, putting his name ahead of hers on the paper's masthead. But, as the owner of and writer on the major African American newspaper in Los Angeles, she participated in community debates about racial issues. Ruth Cowan, hired by United Press to run the Austin, Texas, bureau in 1928, used the name R. Baldwin Cowan when she wrote hard news stories and her full name on human interest features. When higher-ups visited Austin and discovered her gender, they fired her. Cowan went to work for the Associated Press and was given a desk in a separate part of the room from men. "I just got along, that's all," she told an interviewer.[43]

The best approach of all, perhaps, was to flatter men by suggesting that enlightened people did not consider issues such as gender when making hiring decisions. This strategy required a profound understanding of the male ego and of how language, subtly crafted, could shape behavior and ideology. Dorothy Thompson, who spent the early part of the 1920s building a reputation as a foreign correspondent and Berlin bureau chief for the *Philadelphia Public Ledger*, was not generally known for her subtlety. But in a 1926 essay for the progressive magazine, *The Nation*, she demonstrated how well front-page women were learning to use language and cultural stereotypes to their advantage.

Catering to the competitive spirit of Americans, Thompson asserted that they had "an exaggerated interest in all the activities of women, regardless of their intrinsic worth." Europeans, on the other hand, were more sophisticated, according to Thompson. They would "find it curious and amusing that a newspaper woman should take a trip to Europe, at great expense, in order to ascertain what the Queen of the Belgians thinks about love and clothes. But he is not particularly surprised to find a woman interested in the Dawes Plan," she wrote.

Thompson also went to great lengths to present herself as an individual, distancing herself from, as she termed it, the "specious feminism of the women's magazines, which persist in finding cause for jubilation every time a woman becomes . . . an iceman, a road surveyor or a senator." While feminists crowed about women's accomplishments, enlightened men took women's abilities for granted, Thompson assured her readers. "The only question raised, even by the most misogynist males, is whether women can be geniuses. . . . It's high time women were taken for granted."[44]

Along with other female reporters who wrote about their careers in popular magazines and in books, Thompson knew that she had two audiences: the mass audience of readers and the male journalists who made hiring decisions, at her paper and at others. If she made too much of women's recent gains, she risked alienating both audiences and giving male editors an incentive to halt the forward progression of women into newsrooms. Thompson's remarks also make it appear as though she had no interest in advancing the interests of women as a group. But her actions belied her words. She saw herself as a leader whose example could, either positively or negatively, impact other women. And she encouraged other women. Helen Kirkpatrick, who went to work in the 1930s for the *Chicago Daily News*, recalled that Thompson took her under her wing while Kirkpatrick was en route to Europe to become a foreign correspondent.[45]

This same quiet mentoring occurred with other women as well. Bess Furman, an Associated Press reporter who went to work in Washington DC, in the 1920s, recalled in her autobiography that numerous women had mentored her, including Katherine Lewis, "a former crack reporter" for the *St.*

Louis Star Times.[46] The editor of *The Nation* who assigned Dorothy Thompson the essay on female correspondents was a woman, Freda Kirchwey, who frequently used her magazine as a platform to explore women's issues. In a series of articles published in 1926 and 1927, Kirchwey asked women from several fields to explain why they considered themselves feminists. The series was judged to be so controversial that the essays appeared under bylines that read anonymous. Interestingly, a previous series on sexuality had not been nearly as controversial.[47]

The few other women who held positions of authority provided opportunities for female journalists as well. Charlotta Bass of the African American *California Eagle* hired Vera Jackson as a photographer and Fay Jackson (no relation) as a political reporter, sending her to London in 1938 to cover the coronation of King George V. Helen Rogers Reid, publisher of the *New York Herald-Tribune* after the death of her husband, promoted women in every capacity on her paper, sometimes sending them on assignments over the objections of male editors. Gertrude Price, the women's page editor of the *Los Angeles Record*, gave Agness Underwood her first job and pushed her to excel. Years later, when Underwood had become city editor of the *Los Angeles Herald and Express*, she was asked if she favored the hiring of more newspaperwomen. She answered carefully, "More good ones."[48] Mary Neiswender, who went into journalism in the 1940s and became a crack trial reporter at another Los Angeles–area paper, recalled in an interview that, while Underwood did not openly promote women as reporters, she frequently sent congratulatory notes whenever Neiswender wrote a good story.[49]

Women journalists spent the 1920s carefully laying the groundwork for acceptance in front-page journalism. By the 1930s, despite continuing discrimination, they clearly represented a public presence. In 1930, journalist Catharine Oglesby was able to write, in *Ladies Home Journal*, "It is not surprising . . . that newspaper work is so generally regarded as a man's job. Man is, beyond a doubt, the huskier animal of the two." Yet, "notwithstanding the severe tests placed on them, women have arrived in journalism."[50]

Making an Impression: The Depression Years

Between 1920 and 1930, the number of women calling themselves "editors" and "reporters" in the U.S. census more than doubled to 11,920. They represented more than one-quarter of the 39,920 practitioners of journalism.[51] An overwhelming number were white, according to the 1930 census, which listed 76 African American women out of a total of 300 black journalists, a serious undercount. The largest percentage of women journalists were young with nearly half between the ages of twenty and thirty-four. This suggested that many women on the verge of choosing life paths saw journalism as a viable option by the 1930s.[52] And the number of female journalists continued to rise during the 1930s, even during a period when women were strongly discouraged from having any job at all, not to mention careers.

If any specific circumstances are viewed by journalism historians and by female journalists themselves as bringing front-page women more attention and respect in the 1930s, it was the Depression, and the arrival in Washington DC, in March 1933, of Franklin and Eleanor Roosevelt. Volumes have been written about the Roosevelts as shapers of a new political landscape and as political partners in that endeavor. Prominent women's historians have written about Eleanor Roosevelt as a charismatic and unstinting champion of racial equality and as a subtle, but persistent, promoter of gender equality. Journalism historians have emphasized her weekly women-only press conferences and her friendships and alliances with women journalists.[53]

Eleanor Roosevelt played a central role in pushing women front-page reporters into public prominence, but her influence was tacit as well as overt. If women reporters had to learn to play the game of front-page journalism by adapting to the male environment and learning to speak the same language as male reporters, covering national politics gave them a public stage on which to demonstrate mastery of this language – at least in politics.

With her weekly press conferences, Eleanor Roosevelt gave many women the closest access to power they would ever have, and the platform she provided clearly enabled women to write about very serious issues of national import: New Deal programs, unfolding economic developments, and political debates and arguments. Bess Furman of the Associated Press was one of dozens of female journalists who enthusiastically used the forums provided by both Roosevelts. "It was not until years later," she wrote in her autobiography, "that it occurred to me that few women in Washington ever get the opportunity to write of government and political issues as we did."[54] But not all front-page journalists believed that the First Lady's press conferences provided the best public platform for women. Ruth Finney preferred to attend the president's press conferences instead, hoping to suggest, by way of a symbolic gesture to her male colleagues, that she was one of them.[55]

The Depression afforded women journalistic opportunities apart from the venue provided by the Roosevelts and New Deal politics. Americans used the media during this time as an escape hatch, to take them away from the grim realities of their daily lives. People were encouraged to forget their own troubles as they read about the kidnapping of the Lindbergh baby; the birth and early childhood of the Dionne Quintuplets; the abdication of King Edward VIII in England; and the exploits of Amelia Earhart, Babe Didrikson, and other media celebrities. Human interest stories, the kind women were seen as doing best, were now the mainstay of metropolitan journalism and were increasingly brought under the hard news umbrella. Women journalists recognized that audience demand for human interest stories could offer them a larger platform on which to demonstrate their talents. As more women found careers in front-page journalism, the line between hard and soft news began to blur as feature stories shared more and more space on front pages with straightforward accounts of political developments.

During the Depression, male journalists and writers with national reputations – Erskine Caldwell, James Agee, and John Steinbeck among them – provided riveting and vivid stories of people suffering great loss and trauma. Female writers, including Martha Gellhorn and Lorena Hickok, and photographer Margaret Bourke-White, gained national attention and prominence for capturing similar images. Early in the New Deal, Harry Hopkins, who directed the Federal Emergency Relief Administration (FERA), hired both Hickok, a former Associated Press reporter, and Gellhorn, who had written for the *St. Louis Post-Dispatch*, to travel the country documenting the Depression's misery.[56] Bourke-White, who made her reputation in the 1920s working for Henry Luce at *Fortune* magazine, traveled the country in the 1930s as a *Life* magazine photographer.[57]

The realm of "human interest" expanded to include stories of human frailties. Both male and female front-page journalists filled newspapers with stories of insurance scams and schemes that were rampant in Depression-era America. In Los Angeles, Agness Underwood wrote of a church organist who arranged for the murder of his wife by setting up the crime to look like a home invasion robbery. In Boston, reporter Joan Lowell went undercover as a jobless woman for an exposé on urban charities. She described being turned away from a welfare home and from a Salvation Army shelter. By the 1930s female practitioners of this type of journalism, formerly called "sob sisters," were lauded, not denigrated. "My name was emblazoned on billboards and trucks; the public accorded me honors of a heroine; they told me I was courageous, honest, unbeatable, indefatigable," Lowell wrote in her 1933 autobiography, *Gal Reporter.*[58]

For African American women journalists, the Depression offered a different set of professional opportunities. While whites suffered economic deprivation and loss during the 1930s, for blacks, circumstances were far bleaker, both politically and economically. In addition to continuing political oppression and racial terrorism, blacks suffered from higher unemployment rates and had greater difficulty obtaining relief from federal and state agencies. As a result, many black papers began to pressure their communities to boycott white businesses that refused to hire African Americans. As integral leaders in the community, women such as *California Eagle* publisher Charlotta Bass participated prominently in the "Don't Buy Where You Can't Work" campaign, and she published and wrote stories about discrimination on federal relief projects and in local businesses that failed to hire African Americans. But black journalists also pressured their own. At New York's *Amsterdam News*, Marvel Cooke helped to organize the first newspaper guild unit at an African American–owned paper, and she helped to lead the first successful strike of black reporters. The strike taught her that "numbers are power."[59]

The Depression created new ways for women to excel in front-page journalism as they gained a larger audience for their work. This growing audience included readers of newspapers and magazines, writers who published stories about the reporters, book publishers, and filmmakers whose movies began focusing on the exploits of front-page reporters. However, all of these cultural venues ignored the professional accomplishments of African American women and continued the longstanding refusal to see anything outside of white-owned media as culturally significant or interesting.

Between 1930 and 1946, according to Carolyn Galerstein, 130 films featured front-page women as protagonists.[60] Probably the earliest major film is Frank Capra's *Platinum Blonde*, released in 1931 that starred Loretta Young as a reporter who was portrayed as "just one of the guys." Other major films featuring front-page women in the 1930s and 1940s include *Mr. Deeds Goes to Town*, also from Frank Capra, released in 1936; the classic 1940 film *His Girl Friday*, a remake of the 1931 film *The Front Page*, that told the story of male front-page reporters; and *Woman of the Year*, released in 1942, in which Katharine Hepburn played a globe-trotting reporter. Most films were not based specifically on real-life women reporters, but at least two may have been. Marion Sanders, Dorothy Thompson's biographer, suggested that *Woman of the Year* was based on Thompson.[61] And the female photographer, played by Tallulah Bankhead, in 1944's *Lifeboat*, was believed to have been modeled on Margaret Bourke-White.

Reflecting the same mixed messages generally offered by real front-page women, most "reel" front-page women spent a majority of the films demonstrating their competence and professional equality with men, while also suggesting or overtly stating that they believed in more traditional roles. In many, but not all the films, women seemed destined for more traditional roles at the end, but audiences clearly saw capable women on screen, no matter how the stories ended. The same kind of dual message was offered in a 1931 novel by former journalist Mildred Gilman about a front-page woman reporter. The protagonist, a star reporter, loves and excels at her job, but ultimately she heeds the call for marriage and domesticity.[62]

Women seldom acknowledged, publicly at least, the difficulty of maintaining marriage and career, but they hinted at the stresses in Iona Logie's 1935 dissertation on women journalists. In an interview conducted when she was in her eighties, Logie explained her interest in using women journalists as subjects. "From my youth onward, newspapers were always a part of daily reading. Reading the major papers in New York, I became acquainted with the bylines of Ishbel Ross and Emma Bugbee in the *Herald-Tribune*. It occurred to me that a combination of research into a profession, plus my interest in the press, should serve as a useful piece of work."[63]

Logie sent a detailed questionnaire to more than 2,000 female journalists, all of them white, asking about their education, professional experience, earnings, and marital status. The survey was anonymous. Logie received 881 responses. Nearly 50 percent said they worked on newspapers, 28 percent in cities with populations of more than 300,000. Logie did not ask women directly whether they considered themselves front-page reporters, but she included the results of a separate survey of New York female reporters. Out of eighty-four respondents in that survey, nine said they covered hard news. Nearly 50 percent of the respondents to Logie's larger survey were married, and 43.5 percent said they had children.

Not surprisingly, men earned more money than women. Nearly 45 percent of women said they earned between twenty and thirty-two dollars weekly, while another survey of male journalists, cited by Logie, showed only 20 percent of men earned this little. While 43 percent of men earned between thirty-three and sixty dollars weekly, only 28.6 percent of women did so. However, 10.9 percent of women said they earned between sixty-one and one hundred dollars weekly, nearly as many as men, of whom 13.8 percent earned that amount. Women who earned the highest salaries worked for chain newspapers or did national and international reporting.[64]

Logie also compared men's and women's preparation for the field of journalism by asking her female subjects to rank the same factors used in an earlier survey of men. Men rated education and experience as the most important factors in career preparation. Women rated health the most important factor. "I have a constitution like an ox, that's why I can hold out in this job," declared one female respondent.[65]

Asked whether they faced discrimination on the job, 55 percent of women agreed that they did and declared it unjust. When she asked how they had handled it, her respondents seemed to be reading from the same script as Ruth Finney and Emma Bugbee. They downplayed any stereotypical female behavior that could be used against them. But they did not exhibit any traits considered too masculine either. Hence, they reconciled themselves to "working twice as hard (as men)," being "inquiring, but not too inquisitive, persistent, but not obnoxious, sympathetic, but not sentimental; coolly self-possessed but not hard-boiled; independent, but willing to take criticism."[66]

In 1936, Ishbel Ross, the reporter who served as an inspiration for Logie, acknowledged some of these same stresses in her own book on women journalists. They had to be "paradoxical," wrote Ross, "gentle in private life, ruthless at work...."[67] The most successful women, added Ross, were not those who "yipped most loudly about their rights. Unless aggressiveness is backed by real ability . . . it is only a boomerang."[68]

Clearly, Ross herself had learned how to position herself for success in the profession. In the introduction to Ross's book, *New York Herald-Tribune* city editor Stanley Walker declared that Ross represented the male journalist's vision of the ideal woman reporter. She possessed "a lack of giddiness and [a] clear and forthright mind." If that weren't enough, she also demonstrated an "amazing and unfailing stamina on the toughest assignments and calm judgement," according to Walker.[69]

By 1936 women who had succeeded in gaining entrance

to the journalistic fraternity still experienced problems and stresses, but they were earning regard and opportunity, as individuals, in this "compelling profession," suggested Ross.[70] With her "press card opening the way," a woman journalist "walks unscathed through street riots, strikes, fires, catastrophes and revolutions. . . . She watches government in the making, sees presidents inaugurated, kings crowned, heroes acclaimed."[71] Ross was also able to report that, "in spite of the front-page prejudice, every publisher has accepted the fact that he needs a few women on his paper."[72]

Among them was Anne O'Hare McCormick of the *New York Times*, who became the first woman to win a Pulitzer Prize in 1937, for international reporting. But Dorothy Thompson probably best reflects growing male acceptance of women. By the end of the 1930s she was the highest-paid female journalist in America with an annual income topping $100,000. She no longer wrote for the *Philadelphia Public Ledger*, the paper that hired her in the 1920s to cover foreign affairs, but had parlayed her early success into "On the Record," a nationally syndicated column distributed by the *New York Herald-Tribune* and regular radio appearances. She knew how to work on male turf and how to speak to men on their terms, including President Franklin Roosevelt. Divorced from Nobel Prize–winning novelist Sinclair Lewis, she also drank with men and held the floor long into the night at legendary parties she threw at her Vermont farmhouse.[73] Although she was the mother of a son, she spent little time with him and usually left him in the care of others. Nonetheless, in frequent magazine articles, she claimed she longed for domesticity.

Between December 1936 and 1940, Thompson was featured in numerous magazine and newspaper articles that focused on her accomplishments and that gave gender only a bit part in the larger drama of her life and career. Some articles never mentioned gender at all. In December 1936

Thompson was included in a *Saturday Review of Literature* article about six "Personal Journalists" – highly acclaimed opinion-makers. The other five were men: Heywood Broun, Walter Lippmann, Mark Sullivan, Westbrook Pegler, and Hugh S. Johnson. Writer Silas Bent made no mention of Thompson's gender, remarking instead on her liberal political views. Thompson, Lippmann, and Broun, wrote Bent, "represent, and address, in theory at least, that part of our reading public . . . which is vigilant for civil liberty, would curb the excesses of industrial monopoly and finance banking and would like to improve the condition of the under-privileged."[74] Thompson, he continued, "commands as much respect on the part of the reading public, I think, as any other who has turned a hand to political comment."[75] A year later, *Time* magazine featured Thompson on its Books page, noting that she was one of the most popular speakers on the national lecture circuit, commanding $1,000 per speech – higher than any other speaker, including her ex-husband. And, she "turned down 700 invitations to speak."[76]

In May 1940 *The Saturday Evening Post* ran a story on Thompson. The headline over writer Jack Alexander's article called her "The Girl from Syracuse." And Alexander suggested that Thompson's example served as a role for young women, "Miss Thompson furnishes the inspiration which Richard Harding Davis once supplied young men," he noted. But the story focused on her successful career. "Today Miss Thompson is at the forefront of the commentators whose interpretations have in recent years become an indispensable part of the nation's newspaper diet," wrote Alexander. "Miss Thompson's closest competitor among the individual political oracles is Lippmann."[77]

As men finally began to accept women in front-page journalism by the latter years of the 1930s, women themselves began to grow more comfortable and somewhat less cautious in describing themselves and their approach to their jobs. At the same time, their self-descriptions continued to demonstrate how well they had internalized the masculine language of newspapering.

For example, in 1940 when Beverly Smith interviewed Eleanor "Cissy" Patterson, publisher of the *Washington Times-Herald*, she emphasized the stereotypical male attributes that enabled Patterson to thrive. Patterson, a member of the Medill-Patterson family that owned a chain of newspapers, struggled to gain a toehold in journalism until Hearst hired her as editor of the *Washington Herald* in the mid-1930s. In 1939 she bought the paper and combined it with the *Washington Times*. Smith described Patterson as "a born scrapper, loving a fight as dearly as most women love a new evening dress. Whether she is pumping for slum clearance or lambasting the President of the United States, she pulls no punches."[78] Instead of downplaying this aggressive attitude, as front-page women had done for years, however, Patterson herself emphasized the same traits. Describing her attitude, Patterson said, "One can't be a good reporter and a lady at the same time. I'd rather be a reporter."[79]

But this more assertive approach still did not suit everyone. In 1940, Dalia Messick, a female artist using the androgynous first name of Dale, sold the first episode of "Brenda Starr," a comic strip featuring a beautiful red-haired front-page reporter. It quickly became syndicated in newspapers throughout the country. Throughout its long history, the strip always emphasized Starr's beauty and femininity more than her professional skills when it came to her numerous scoops.[80]

Although films, book publishers, and magazine writers ignored the work of African American women throughout the 1930s, they too had made significant inroads in front-page journalism by the end of the decade. Like white women, they had learned to adapt themselves to masculine rules and then use the platform journalism provided to carve out their own niches. In the 1920s, the *California Eagle* was a small paper published by Charlotta Bass and her husband, Joseph Bass. It had little discernable political philosophy and contained a confusing mass of stories that included news about social events, church activities, advertising, and local and national politics. Charlotta Bass deferred publicly to her husband, while writing most of the stories and traveling widely.

In 1934 Joseph Bass died and his widow stepped confidently into the limelight. She labored diligently to make her paper important in the larger struggle for civil rights. In addition to playing a strong role in the national "Don't Buy Where You Can't Work" campaign, she started a Los Angeles radio program and promoted herself as a speaker at African American political and social organizations throughout the state of California. In New York, meanwhile, Marvel Cooke moved from the *Amsterdam News* to the left-leaning *People's Voice*, where she wrote front-page stories and helped to edit the paper. She became managing editor in 1940.[81]

While the career paths and strategies of black women resembled those of white women, moving ahead in their chosen profession required the ability to become instrumental in shaping political changes that affected the entire community. Cooke accomplished this through union activism; Bass continually reminded male leaders in Los Angeles that she controlled the instrument that gave African Americans a presence in Los Angeles. "Believe it or not, the newspaper is your weapon against discrimination . . . against political and social oppression, against the million and one problems . . . which Americans of color face today," she wrote in a front-page column in the early 1940s.[82]

World War II and Women Front-Page Journalists
By the 1940s, black and white women had positioned themselves as unique individuals rather than the vanguard of a larger group of women aiming at nontraditional careers in

front-page journalism. This success paved the way for women to surmount the last significant barrier standing in the way of their acceptance: the belief that they were unequipped to cover the brutality and horrors of war.

By the 1940 census, 14,750 women claimed journalism as their occupation, 3,000 more than a decade earlier; this was a somewhat surprising statistic considering the fate of many women workers in the Depression. In 1940 women represented 25 percent of the journalistic profession. Their median age was 37.4, suggesting that most women hired the previous decade had managed to keep their jobs. But younger women clearly found jobs as well. The largest cohort, 5,387 women, was between the ages of twenty-five and thirty-four, and 2,350 women were under the age of twenty-five. As in the previous decade's census, the numbers suggested an overwhelmingly white profession, citing only 115 African American women, an increase of nearly 50 percent, out of a total of 391 black journalists.[83]

If World War I cracked open the newsroom door to women and the Depression opened it wider, World War II finally demonstrated that women belonged in front-page journalism. "How the young wage earners take the privilege of a job for granted," columnist Marie Manning wrote in 1944. Manning, who had worked as an advice columnist for Pulitzer at the turn of the century, noted that, "Who of us, in those early days, would have dreamed of tackling a political figure on a political subject? Newswomen have almost forgotten when we had to limit ourselves to discussions of puddings and petticoats."[84]

The Second World War was significant for women front-page journalists because it opened up jobs on two fronts – at home, replacing men who left to fight, and overseas, as war correspondents. To say that many men, by the end of World War II, had acquiesced to the notion that women might be emotionally and physically equipped to work in newsrooms is not to suggest that all barriers had fallen. Women still experienced discrimination on assignments. They were paid less than men, and city editors still said to job applicants, "We already have one woman." But it was one more than many papers had twenty or even ten years earlier.

A few women had been correspondents in past wars – going all the way back to the mid-nineteenth century and Margaret Fuller, who covered the Italian Revolution for the *New York Tribune* in the 1840s. But World War II represented the first time that women "covered the war at the front on a par with men."[85] Women were prepared to tackle this assignment when the war began because a few of them were stationed overseas and were writing about looming conflicts in China, Germany, Italy, and the Soviet Union. They included Ruth Gruber, who during the 1930s worked her way into a foreign correspondent's job with the *New York Herald-Tribune* and reported from the Soviet Union. "Journalism helped me become a participant and witness in events that would change the world forever," Gruber wrote in her memoirs.[86] Because of their overseas experience, women like Gruber had already demonstrated their mettle when the United States entered the war in December 1941. Nonetheless, it took nearly a year for the War Department to agree to officially accredit women war correspondents. About a hundred women ultimately gained this accreditation.[87]

World War II was a crucial proving ground for women because theaters of war had long been viewed as the ultimate male space and far more heavily guarded than the newsroom had ever been. Women knew that breaking down the walls of this fortified stronghold would surely hasten the demise of the old, now weakened argument that women could not compete with men in front-page news. But they knew they had to walk the same ground as men to succeed, to demonstrate that they were equal to their male counterparts both to the audience of their peers and to a larger, mass audience at home reading the newspapers and magazines.

The public attention given to women war correspondents helped to draw even more women into journalism during the 1940s. During this decade the number of women journalists more than doubled, to about 30,000, and by 1950 they represented 32 percent of the profession. The number of black women journalists also doubled in the 1940s, according to the census, which listed 222 women, out of a total of 568 black journalists.[88]

Covering war may have been the most masculine of enterprises, but female journalists were not alone in crossing heretofore rigidly enforced gender boundaries during this conflict. Women pilots, female major league baseball players, symphony orchestra members, and Rosie the Riveters also used wartime exigencies to help to reshape the terms of debate about gender. Again, as throughout the entire interwar period, women journalists provided the most public examples of gender-bending. Most of the women in other fields were only filling in on a wartime basis. Front-page women were the only women, besides nurses, who actually went to war.

Gaining a coveted wartime assignment from the federal government and from editors and publishers was a difficult enterprise. First, front-page women journalists had to obtain the permission of publishers and editors to go overseas. Then they had to undergo rigorous screening by the War Department. Ruth Cowan, who covered the war in Europe and North Africa for the Associated Press, recalled being asked by a War Department interviewer whether she was athletic, afraid of firearms, and able to keep a secret. He also told her she would not be comfortable. Despite the rugged conditions, women war correspondents had to wear uniforms that included skirts as well as pants.[89]

From their first moments at the front, women had to

demonstrate that they could carry their own weight, recalled Cowan. They could not expect men to "be gallant."[90]
Or even polite. Cowan's own ability to adapt herself to wartime circumstances emerged in an interview she gave long
after the war. She described how she reacted when Wes
Gallagher, head of the Associated Press bureau in North Africa, refused to assign her any stories because he did not
want a woman attached to his unit. So Cowan found her
own stories, focusing on the human angle of war. For one
story she went behind the lines to write about an evacuation
hospital in the mountains of Tunisia. During press briefings
by the military, Cowan always stood in the back of the room.
"I didn't want to get thrown out," she recalled.[91]

Other women adopted this same independent approach.
"I never moved with a group of women," declared Helen
Kirkpatrick, who covered the war in Europe and North Africa for the *Chicago Daily News*.[92] Kirkpatrick was so well
thought of by her journalistic peers that they selected her
as the only woman to help plan media coverage of D-Day in
1944.[93] Discussing herself and reporter Martha Gellhorn,
Kirkpatrick noted, "We had been newspaper people before
the war and didn't need to be led around in a group."[94] In
Italy, Kirkpatrick lived in a muddy nurses' tent – close to an
enemy encampment – and with a rudimentary latrine,
walled off by a blanket. In addition to writing her stories, she
helped the nurses care for their patients.[95]

Some women who eventually became noted war correspondents took advantage of the fact that the military was
drafting men in order to get jobs in stateside newsrooms.
Marguerite Higgins was one of them and her experience illustrates the changing climate for front-page women by the
1940s. Unlike women who had entered the profession
twenty, or even ten, years earlier, Higgins, hired by the *New
York Herald-Tribune* in 1942, was not willing to present herself as the "paradox" recommended by Ishbel Ross in *Ladies*

of the Press. Higgins, both professionally and privately, was outspokenly competitive and aggressive – in other words, stereotypically male. From the beginning, she proved willing to do anything to get a story, including sleeping with sources and stealing copy from the typewriters of her competitors. "I obviously had a strong competitive drive instilled in me very early," she acknowledged in her autobiography. "In newspaper work, fear of the second-best clearly serves as a powerful prod."[96] Although many of Higgins's colleagues disliked and complained about her, their attitude had little or no effect on her career. She went on to win a Pulitzer Prize for covering the Korean War in the 1950s.

Higgins's experience also illustrates how well the unspoken female network of mentoring worked, even for someone who exhibited such "male" behavior. In fall 1944 after two years in the *Herald-Tribune* newsroom, Higgins asked women's page editor Dorothy Dunbar Bromley to try to convince publisher Helen Reid to send her to Europe to cover the war. Although Higgins was far down the list of hopefuls – including many men – Bromley "plugged for me with no other motive than a conviction that I would do a good job."[97] Reid agreed to send her, and she arrived in Europe just a few months before the war ended.

In Europe Higgins's fearlessness and aggressiveness served her well. In April 1945 she covered the retreat of the German Army and the liberation of the concentration camps. At Dachau at the end of April 1945, she joined up with a male *Stars and Stripes* reporter. Taking a jeep behind the lines, the pair reached the camp before the military and ordered the German commanders to surrender to them. As she reported in the *Herald-Tribune*, the prisoners who were able to walk began flinging themselves against the electric fences, and she had to plead with them, in German, to stop. "I didn't have enough sense to be afraid," she wrote in her autobiography.[98]

Women may have faced skepticism and disapproval from official sources throughout the war, but the public clearly accepted them by 1945, if popular magazines are any indication. In March 1945, *Newsweek* magazine carried a laudatory article about three women correspondents – Iris Carpenter of the *Boston Globe*, Ann Stringer of United Press, and Lee Carson of International News Service. The article noted approvingly that the three women had managed to circumvent the military's requirement that they stay away from the front. The military, wrote *Newsweek*, believed that "the presence of women upfront distracts the soldier. But the three correspondents have disproved this. They asked no favors and gave none. They dug their own foxholes and took front-line life without complaint."[99]

For African American female front-page journalists, World War II also represented a professional watershed. An article in the African American magazine *Opportunity* – discussing women's roles in general – suggests how much attitudes had changed since World War I. "The desire for careers was very evident during the '20s," wrote George DeMar. "Frustration snapped at the heels of many during the '30s. Today, at the beginning of the '40s, for many Negro women the idea of a 'career' . . . looms for the first time as a reality."[100]

Although no sources identify them as war correspondents, black women journalists played crucial roles, along with their male colleagues, in pointing out the disjuncture between the democratic credo of America and reality for black people during World War II. The national "Double V for Victory" program, promoted by most of the major black newspapers, linked continuing racism at home with the fight against fascism abroad. Publishers and editors risked their livelihoods by participating in the program, coming under intense surveillance by the federal government and the FBI, which overtly and subtly threatened the ability of black papers to continue publishing unless they stopped challenging racial brutality and discriminatory practices in the military and in industry.[101]

Ironically, the "Double V for Victory" program brought the black press much more exposure in the white, mainstream media than it had received previously. And much of it was positive in tone. A 1943 article in *The New Republic* and two 1942 articles in the *Saturday Review of Literature* attempted to explain the "Negro Press" to readers. An April 26, 1943, *New Republic* article noted that, "The race press has grown up to fill a need as important to the Negro as the home-town paper to any white man. Since the World War, it has become an important implement of the Negro minority in making its pressure effective."[102] Daisy Bates of Little Rock, Arkansas, and Charlotta Bass of Los Angeles were two African American woman journalists for whom anti-discrimination crusades during the war brought wider public exposure. Both went on, after the war, to take national leadership positions, in their own rights, on civil rights struggles.

Bates and her husband, L. C. Bates, established the *Arkansas State Press* in 1941. "Our decision was based on the conviction that a newspaper was needed to carry on the fight for Negro rights as nothing else can," she wrote in her autobiography, *The Long Shadow of Little Rock*. With the onset of war thousands of soldiers crowded into a nearby military base, Camp Robinson. Police frequently attacked black soldiers who came into town on weekend leave. Although the *State Press* crusaded against police brutality, the issue simmered beneath the surface until March 1942 when a white policeman murdered a black soldier. In editorials and dozens of front-page articles, Bates castigated the town and its police force, earning the enmity of the white political and business establishment. "From this beginning, the *State Press* expanded its crusading role on an ever widening front," wrote

Bates. "It fought to free Negroes from muddy, filthy streets, slum housing, menial jobs and injustice in the court-rooms."[103] After the war, Bates became a tireless crusader for civil rights in Little Rock as a leader of the NAACP In 1957 she was the catalyst behind the successful effort to integrate Central High School.

By World War II Charlotta Bass had been publishing and writing for the *California Eagle* for thirty years. She was so well known that in 1940 she was named as a regional direc-tor of Republican presidential candidate Wendell Willkie's campaign. But the war catapulted her onto the national stage as a more prominent supporter of racial equality and justice. Bass was an avid proponent of the "Double V for Vic-tory" program, and her paper continuously printed articles criticizing the government and pointing out ongoing dis-crimination and brutality toward blacks. Despite being vis-ited more than once by FBI agents, she refused to stop print-ing critical stories. One of her most rigorous campaigns was against restrictive covenants – the practice of requiring homebuyers or sellers in white neighborhoods in Los Ange-les to agree not to sell to African Americans or other racial minorities.

Despite all of her strong criticisms, she avidly supported the American effort in World War II. But in 1945, after her nephew died fighting the war in Europe, she began to openly question the American political system and to focus on creating a coalition of working class African Americans and whites throughout the world. By the end of the war, Bass had stopped catering to the egos of male leaders and was moving toward a radical vision of social change that made her a target of the FBI for the remainder of her life.

Between the ends of World War I and World War II, women front-page journalists played a crucial role in helping to change the terms of debate about gender. Their personal examples and ubiquitous bylines on every kind of story could not help but shatter stereotypes and affect their audience's perception of women's inherent qualities and prescribed roles. To break down these longstanding stereotypes and prejudices, the women had to walk a narrow tightrope, always conscious that if they slipped, they would hinder the ability of other women to follow in their footsteps. Each woman had to adopt her own individual strategy, depending on her personality and circumstances. But all had to learn to adapt themselves to the rules and the language of the men who set the terms, both in larger society and in the field of journalism itself. Their success in reaching out to a mass audience is reflected in film depictions of women who used the exact same language and exhibited the exact same professional qualities they presented – women working as "newspapermen."

It also is reflected in the words of India McIntosh, a front-page reporter who went to work at the *New York Herald-Tribune* in 1931 with a "timid smile and a few modest exaggerations about my ability." By 1947, she wrote, women journalists had "so softened up the opposing forces that the battle is a mock one." As proof, McIntosh offered up the story of a ship explosion in the New York harbor. Journalists converged on the scene, piling into trucks to take them to the disaster site. McIntosh and another women reporter jumped into one truck with twenty male reporters. A shore patrolman flagged the truck to a stop, telling the driver: "No women allowed on this pier." Before the women could say anything, a male photographer responded, "These aren't women, they're reporters."[104]

Ruth Finney with Scripps Howard
coworkers in 1931. That year Scripps
Howard nominated Finney for a
Pulitzer Prize for her investigative
reporting of the power industry.
Courtesy of the Department of Special Collections, University of California Library, Davis, California.

2. Journey from the Star

The Life and Work of Ruth Finney

In October 1937 a San Francisco radio station broadcast an interview with Ruth Finney, one of the most prominent women reporters in Washington DC. Interviewer Janet Baird started out by taking note of the popular film image of front-page women as "wisecracking girl reporters." She then declared that real women reporters faced decidedly more difficult circumstances than their "reel" counterparts. Only a handful of women had reached the top echelons of reporting, she noted, where they were viewed as the equals of "ace men reporters." Finney, who worked for Scripps Howard News Alliance, was one such journalist.

The interview focused on Finney's rise in journalism, beginning in 1922 when she scooped the rest of the world on a mine disaster in Jackson, California, in which forty-seven men died. Baird discussed Finney's coverage of many high-profile stories: Nicola Sacco and Bartolomeo Vanzetti, Italian immigrants convicted and executed for killing a Massachusetts paymaster; the Bonus Army March; the building of Hoover Dam; malfeasance in the power industry and federal efforts to regulate the industry.

Baird also asked Finney about First Lady Eleanor Roosevelt's press conferences, which had opened up a new world of opportunity for women journalists in the nation's capital. Finney described Roosevelt's first press conference, held in March 1933. "Reporters sat cross-legged like Girl Scouts," she said. "Mrs. Roosevelt passed out cookies and no one knew what to ask." She admitted, however, that she seldom attended Eleanor Roosevelt's press conferences, but added, "I rarely miss one of the president's."

When Baird asked Finney to discuss her numerous scoops, she demurred, declaring they had happened mostly "by accident." She also turned the conversation to her husband, journalist Robert S. Allen, co-writer with Drew Pearson of the popular syndicated political column, "Washington Merry-Go-Round." "He's much more important than I am."[1] This was Finney's public persona – modest and interested in letting her audience know she was serious, not frivolous; traditional enough to be married, but not traditional enough to take her husband's name, to quit her job after marriage, or to attend press conferences with women rather than men. Those listening at home might have seen her as a path breaker, but not as a threat to the status quo. They might also have concluded that her male editors and colleagues thought enough of her to give her good assignments and to welcome her into their gatherings, but that she was deferential enough to stay in the background.

Much the same image of Finney emerges from newspaper and magazine articles written about her during her forty-seven-year career. She carefully cut out and saved many of the articles. Front-page reporter Ishbel Ross, who in 1936 wrote perhaps the most definitive book on women in journalism to date, referred to Finney as "the best newspaperwoman I have ever known. She doesn't look it. Slim, red hair always smooth, conspicuously immaculate in subtly simple costumes, to meet her is to recall calm saints in stained glass windows, hushed cathedral aisles." Ross went on to describe Finney as an intellectual. Adding, however, that "her vigor is masked behind a quiet feminine manner."[2]

But the public Ruth Finney was not the same as the private Ruth Finney. A different side of her personality emerged in the date books and diaries she kept from the 1910s to 1942. These sources reflect a woman grateful for the professional opportunities she received yet frustrated with gender inequalities, proud of her accomplishments, and fiercely competitive. She frequently congratulated herself about scoops, sometimes adding an exclamation point for emphasis. About the Argonaut Mine disaster, which became her first important exclusive story, Finney wrote in her August 28, 1922, diary, "Sleeping with my clothes on, jumping up at odd hours to ride up to the mouth of the Argonaut. I've never competed with the cream of the crop (in journalism) before." Three weeks later, still waiting to discover the fate of the miners, Finney wrote, "The whole thing is hell for almost everyone else involved, but for me, it's something I wouldn't have missed."[3]

Throughout her career, Finney wrote privately about her anger at pay inequities and other symbols of gender discrimination. In fact, she seems to have been exceptionally sensitive about these issues, noting in her diary each time her pay was raised or cut, as it was during the Depression. "Sore – found out boss going to pay Max Stern more for same job," she wrote to her diary in 1930.[4] Seven years later, after reading an article in *Literary Digest* that pegged her salary at $12,000 a year, she wrote, "Exactly twice what I earn and probably indicates what men in similar jobs are being paid."[5] However, her annual salary matched almost exactly the average, $5,987, noted in a 1935 survey of Washington correspondents.[6]

Finney also privately reveled in "firsts" for other women as well as herself. About Frances Perkins, Franklin Roosevelt's Labor Secretary and America's first female cabinet member, she wrote in her March 12, 1933, diary, "She can have me for a doormat anytime. She appeared before a joint Senate and House Committee yesterday and made the men who were questioning her look like the dimwits they are."[7] Although she declared herself a loner, Finney joined the Women's National Press Club and enjoyed writing skits aimed at puncturing the egos of powerful males for the annual dinner designed to rival the men-only National Press Club's gridiron dinner. In 1932 she took the wife of California senator Hiram Johnson to the WNPC dinner, where she had written a skit parodying the United States Senate as needing medical attention to deal with the arrival of Hattie Caraway, a female senator from Arkansas.[8]

Her diaries indicate that she connected strongly with women's issues, although she never overtly proclaimed herself a feminist. She had a female doctor, her closest female friend was journalist Ruby Black, an avowed feminist who operated her own wire service in Washington DC, and she wrote glowingly about other successful women. In December 1924 she wrote an article on Alice Roosevelt Longworth, the controversial daughter of former President Theodore Roosevelt. "None of your dull stodgy stuff about her . . . Oh no. Alice would leap onto the back of the sacred elephant standing in front of the temple and ride him around a little, then slide down. . . . What a story it made."[9] In a February 1936 diary entry, she mentioned writing an article on historian Mary Beard, "who said men have neglected things women have done."[10]

Finney's professional success provides strong evidence that she recognized the power she could gain as a female reporter by maintaining careful control of her own image, particularly during the early years when she was proving herself to an audience composed of colleagues, bosses, and readers. In some ways, she had to be two different people: in private, ferociously competitive, and in public, a person who performed in front of a large audience. In this latter role, she took great care not to offend or to say anything that might raise questions about women's roles and her own part in helping to enlarge them. This strategy brought respect and admiration from her peers. In 1931 Finney's male editors at Scripps Howard nominated her for a Pulitzer Prize for her coverage of the electric power industry. If she had won she would have been the first woman so honored. It took six more years for a woman, *New York Times* reporter Anne McCormick, to win journalism's top prize, but Finney's nomination nonetheless signaled her arrival in front-page journalism.

The need to hide her ambition and competitiveness behind a veil of deference and modesty exacted a price. She acknowledged as much throughout her diary by making frequent references to illness usually in conjunction with some stress in her career or personal life. In July 1928 when her editor denied her desire to ride on the Herbert Hoover presidential campaign train and chose to send a male reporter instead, Finney wrote, "Intestinal flu, sick, three degrees of fever."[11] She was again sick during her courtship with Robert Allen in early 1929, and she talked openly about her fear of matrimony.[12] In late 1935, when she learned she would get a new editor, Finney wrote, "sick, lost nine pounds."[13]

Despite all of the stress, however, she believed the effort was worth it. And she understood how important her struggles had been in helping to reshape larger cultural ideas about gender roles. She acknowledged as much in an account of her career, "Journey from the *Star*," written after she retired from Scripps Howard but never published. "The unusual opportunity [the profession] offered to a woman justifies leaving a record of it," she noted in her autobiography. Completed in 1973, six years before her death, the manuscript proudly details how she set out to be a teacher but fell "in love at first sight" with "the ordered confusion, deadlines, informality of newspapering in the summer of 1918" when she walked in the door of the *Sacramento Star*, a small but scrappy newspaper in California's capital city.[14]

But as her autobiography makes clear, she was a front-page reporter not a reporter who wrote features or society stories. "This is the account of newspaper work by a woman reporter specializing in politics and public affairs," she wrote.[15] No matter how she chose to present it in public, her career did not just happen. She was an intensely ambitious woman, although she hid her ambition beneath a surface of femininity and an apparent willingness, particularly in the early years of her career, to cover any type of story and to do it so well that no one could question her ability or her gender.

From California to Washington

Ruth Finney was born in March 1898 in Downieville, a small mountain town in Northern California, where she spent her childhood. Her parents were both widowed. Her father was fifty-five and her mother almost forty when she was born, and she was their only child. Although political reporting was not considered a job option for women at the time, her later career focus seems a natural fit; Finney's childhood was shaped by politics. In 1906, in his sixties, her father, John Finney, a mine superintendent, won election to the California State Legislature as a Republican. But in 1908 he was defeated by the railroad interests that had long held California politicians in a viselike grip. Two years after her father's defeat, Hiram Johnson won the election as a reforming, progressive governor who promised to rid the state of special interests.[16] Finney subsequently followed Johnson's career very closely and eventually became a close friend, until Johnson broke with Franklin Roosevelt in the late 1930s over preparedness for World War II.

Finney was fourteen when her father died, and she and her mother left their small town to live in Sacramento. Her mother used her connections with state lawmakers to get a job as postmistress to the state legislature. Ruth helped her run a boardinghouse to make extra money when the legislature was not in session. The two women remained extremely close and lived together until the end of Mary Finney's life in the 1930s.

In 1916, her last year of high school, Ruth was one of six students who earned a scholarship to the San Jose Normal School, a teacher training facility. After spending two years in San Jose, south of San Francisco, she moved back to Sacramento in the summer of 1918, planning to teach elementary school. But fate intervened. Bert Hews, editor of the *Sacramento Star* and a friend of her family's, asked if she could fill in at the newspaper until school started. In the midst of World War I, most available men had enlisted and had gone to Europe.

As Finney recalled fifty years later, Hews looked the part of the stereotypical newspaperman, "with a cigar and green eye shade." He offered her ten dollars a week. The newsroom was "sweltering and windowless," and she was given "a chair with no back, a table and a ratty old typewriter and phone," and was told to make calls to the undertaker. Her male colleagues used "profanity I had never heard before."[17] At the end of her two-week stint Finney faced a quandary. She wanted to stay at the newspaper, but her mother believed teaching was a more proper female profession and also more secure. Ruth solved her problem by trying to do both jobs – reporting and substitute teaching. "Taught second grade – very, very unhappy," she reported in September 1918. "I want to be a journalist so badly."[18] By the end of the month, she decided to take a leap of faith and abandon teaching.

The *Star*, part of the twenty-paper Scripps Howard chain, was the smallest of three newspapers in California's capital city in the early twentieth century. Talented writers and editors frequently left the *Star* for the *Sacramento Union* or the *Sacramento Bee*, which were much more prestigious and profitable papers. The *Bee* later bought the *Star* from Scripps Howard. Because the paper was small, Finney was able to learn all aspects of the newspaper business, from laying out pages to setting type, taking photos, and reporting stories. She covered a wide variety of assignments – city politics, urban corruption, court trials – that would have gone to male reporters on larger papers. She also wrote editorials promoting the city manager form of government and railed against the Ku Klux Klan. By 1920 she earned thirty-four dollars a week, and in 1922 she became city editor, directing the newsroom operation and editing the copy of her male colleagues. She may have acted the part of a hard-news journalist, but she looked more like a schoolmarm, wearing on one occasion "a long white silk dress with sprigs of blue flowers, a lace collar and bonnet trimmed with silk rosebuds." The dress was covered with an apron, she added, to ward off ink stains.[19]

Shortly after her promotion to city editor, Finney's career rocketed on an upward trajectory with "the scoop of a lifetime," as she later phrased it. In August 1922 a mine collapsed in Jackson, about sixty miles southeast of Sacramento, and trapped forty-seven miners 4,350 feet below the earth's surface. Although she should have sent a reporter, Finney argued that her mining background made her the paper's ideal choice for covering the story. United Press, a wire service that had the *Sacramento Star* as a client, asked her to provide copy for it as well; this connection would give her stories a statewide audience. The rescue effort lasted more than three weeks, and Finney was one of more than one hundred reporters who crowded into the small, dusty town amid searing heat and smoldering resentment of journalists. Residents "united in hatred" of the reporters, she wrote in her autobiography. The reporters "drank, laughed and were offensive. They were demanding and thoughtless and engaged in light-hearted banter in the midst of tragedy."[20]

Finney took a room in the town's single hotel and made

daily and nightly trips to the mine. To ensure that she would be on top of any eventuality, she decided to write two stories in advance of the rescue – one if the men were found alive and one if they were found dead. She thought a Biblical reference would be appropriate and so scoured the town for a Bible. "The final two days and nights were exhausting," she recalled. "I had no sleep, one sandwich and one donut." The discovery that all the miners had died came while Finney was talking to her editor on the only phone line available to reporters. "My boss called on the sawmill phone. I saw (another reporter) running toward the mill and kept the line open. We got the news that all of the miners were probably dead." She held onto the phone and began dictating one of her prewritten stories.[21] Tragically sentimental, her report was in the "sob sister" vein using the resurrection of Jesus as a reference point:

Very early in the morning, women of Jackson came to the shaft of the Kennedy mine where their men were buried. And they found the stone cleared away from the shaft. And they waited while men entered the shaft, but found not their husbands and their brothers.[22]

Another Finney story about the disaster read:

Jackson mourned its dead today. The little city brought three weeks of hopeful waiting to an end last night, and this morning was plunged deeper and deeper into gloom as the realization of tragedy grew upon it. "They got the 47."[23]

The scoop of a lifetime earned Finney a 100 percent raise in salary and the admiration and respect of her peers. By the spring of 1923 she had moved on to the *San Francisco Star*, a bigger Scripps Howard paper. There she covered the unexpected death of President Warren G. Harding in that city. Her story about Mrs. Harding was again aimed at wringing emotion from readers: "Walk into the blackness of the valley of the shadow with her if you can. Send your spirit a little way with hers – that wife whose soul is rocked with agony today. Perhaps it can reach her through the darkness."[24] By the end of 1923 Finney was on her way to Washington DC; she had been hired by the Scripps Howard News Alliance to cover national politics for its seven western papers – four in California and one each in Arizona, New Mexico, and Colorado. Editors of papers in San Diego and Los Angeles requested that she focus most of her reporting on the effort to get the federal government to build a dam on the Colorado River.

The first articles written about Finney began appearing in 1923 and focused on her work during the Argonaut Mine disaster. The writer of one article mentioned her gender and noted that she was "the only girl trusted" by male editors to report the story. Finney responded by declaring her gratitude "for the $10 [weekly] offer that started me as a cub reporter." When the writer mentioned other stories Finney wrote, including a series aimed at reforming city government, Finney responded modestly, "It was worth the work. It's delightful to feel that you've done your part toward a reform."[25]

Reading this article and others in the same vein, it is possible to believe that her good fortune simply happened. Left unsaid was how she had wangled her way into the mine disaster assignment, positioned herself by the telephone in Jackson, and refused to abandon it so that other reporters could phone in their own stories. Or how she was already prepared with two stories, rather than leaving her dictating skills to chance. She may have appeared modest to her interviewer, but to her diary she took careful note of her status as the only "serious" woman reporter in Jackson. The *San Francisco Chronicle* had sent Marjorie Driscoll, Finney wrote, but she was "a feature writer."[26] In fact, this was an inaccurate depiction of Driscoll, who became a prominent Hearst reporter in Los Angeles.

Finney seems always to have viewed herself as destined for important things, although she may never have acknowledged this publicly. She wrote novels and submitted articles and short stories, virtually all unpublished, to Sacramento newspapers while still in her teens. "I'd give anything to be in Chicago (at a political convention)," she wrote to her diary during the summer she was eighteen. Although she attended a teacher preparation college in San Jose, this was not a profession that really excited her, and she struggled with ambition for other fields throughout her tenure at the San Jose school. At one point after she "made an impromptu speech from the platform and was highly commended," she exulted, "Maybe the lawyer ambition is not so impractical."[27] The following winter, after attending a talk on China and India at the YMCA, she wrote, "The people who *do* things and go places *fascinate* me."[28]

Finney's aspirations and her views about gender are apparent in several novels she wrote throughout her life. None were published, possibly because they were written in stilted prose, had plodding plots, and generally lacked conflict or color. But all provide strong evidence of her belief that women were strong and capable and that they should be able to do anything that they wanted. In "To G. H. from B.," written when she was eighteen, Finney told the story of a schoolteacher who, after discovering a plot to steal a friend's money, succeeded single-handedly in thwarting both the elements and the villain to make everything all right. Derisively discussing one of her students, the schoolteacher declares that "she hasn't learned as yet to think of any kind of a future that does not include marriage."[29] In "Lady Boss," written sometime in the 1930s or 1940s, Finney told the story of a front-page reporter remarkably like herself. She breaks up a gambling ring, is elevated to city editor, takes badgering and insults from her all-male staff, and still succeeds in unearthing corruption in city government. Her protagonist in this story did choose to marry in the end but unlike some novelistic and film portrayals of women journalists at this time, only in combination with a career.[30]

As these stories demonstrate Finney was confident that she would succeed professionally despite longstanding prejudices about women. This can be seen in many diary entries. Editor Bert Hews "said I was the best cub reporter he'd ever seen," she noted after her first few days on the job at the *Star*. A month later she predicted that "our paper is soon going to put the *Bee* and the (Sacramento) *Union* out of business." In November 1920, while she was researching her series on urban reform, Finney took note of a businessman who "told me I knew more about municipal government than anyone in Sacramento."[31]

But she recognized that gender would be a factor that could help and hinder her. It could attract attention as a novelty, but it could also keep her from getting jobs. For this reason perhaps she was extremely conservative in her appearance and clothing. She wore her long hair pinned up and often covered with a stylish hat. During the years she kept her diary she referred frequently to tasteful dresses she bought and wore on the job. For example, regarding a 1932 press club party she wrote, "I had a new white dress with wide, dark blue velvet sash. $16.50."[32] At a 1928 national political convention held in Houston, Texas, at the height of summer, she noted to her diary that all the other women attending "went about in short-sleeved dresses." Despite the oppressive heat, she continued wearing long sleeves. "It didn't seem proper to me to go about the streets and to the convention hall, in such informal clothes," she wrote.[33]

Although her outward demeanor was modest and proper, she could be ferocious in pursuit of her career goals. Finney left the *Sacramento Star* because the paper's owner refused to make her editor-in-chief. She was only twenty-five at the time. "They just don't want a woman," she grumbled to her

diary in January 1923. "As if I haven't been doing everything
there is to do."[34] Six months later, working for the San Francisco paper, she complained, "They have me doing feature
stories, sob sister style and I would rather be doing something solid, like politics."

Just before leaving for Washington DC, Finney's editors
assigned her to write a story on an Oakland charm school.
"Ugh," was her one-word response to her diary.[35] As she prepared to leave for Washington Finney debated whether she
would ever come back to San Francisco to work. "I'd like to
count for more in SF when I do come back," she told her diary. "I haven't been as important here . . . as I was to the (Sacramento) *Star*."[36]

A Woman Reporter in Washington

When Finney arrived in Washington, "a woman reporter
was an oddity in press galleries," she wrote in her diary. Despite this fact she immediately began to get good stories. She
made a strategic decision at this point to focus on only serious stories that would earn her respect from men. The Tea-
pot Dome scandal is a case in point. The case involved Secretary of the Interior Albert Fall, who was accepting bribes
from oil companies in exchange for offering them leases to
public oil lands. Finney said she got the assignment because
of its western angle. Fall was from New Mexico, the location
of one of her client papers. Edward Doheny, the wealthy
oilman who bribed government officials, was from California, the location of Elk Hills, one of the sites of the oil leases.
She proudly boasted of the nickname Fall's attorney, Frank
Hogan, coined for her, "Poison Ivy," in reference to the hard-
hitting and harshly critical stories she wrote on the case.[37] By
June 1926 she was earning one hundred dollars weekly, a remarkably high salary for either women or men at the time.[38]

It was the debate over electric power that earned Finney
her national reputation. She began covering the story in the

late 1920s because all of her client papers insisted she do so. Finney approached the story like a dog that would not let go of a trouser leg, covering every arcane detail of the complex issue. Her papers were specifically interested in the ongoing struggle to control the Colorado River. In 1922 the seven western states that shared the river tried but failed to reach agreement on water usage. A bill authored by Senator Hiram Johnson and Congressman Phil Swing, both from California, sought to build a dam in Boulder Canyon that would store water and provide electrical power to western states.

It took six years of unrelenting lobbying to get the bill through both houses of Congress. An agreement had to be worked out for a compact among the states; Swing and Johnson had to overcome an effort by power industry representatives to replace a proposed large dam for electric power with a smaller, water-supplying facility; and they had to get approval for $125 million – later $165 million – in bonds to pay for dam construction. In 1926 the bill was voted out of the Senate Committee on Irrigation and Reclamation, and in 1927, on the floor of the House of Representatives, Swing had to explain all over again why a dam was necessary. Opponents from the power industry prompted a filibuster in the Senate that lasted more than thirty hours in 1927. Finally, in 1928, the bill passed both houses.[39]

Finney's coverage of the story gave her editors more than they ever could have hoped for. She made herself an expert on the power industry and its players. "The story was mostly my own," she acknowledged in her autobiography.[40] That this was so had to do with the subject – technical, arcane, and not particularly exciting or amenable to explanation with a few pithy quotes. It took someone patient, dogged, and willing to follow it over a period of years. Finney was that person. Her diary offers strong evidence that she intentionally carved out this niche as a way of gaining attention. In August 1928 she lunched with a male journalist who offered her career advice. "He suggested I study all there is about power and write a book on it."[41]

Covering the story required intense dedication. Finney described a typical day: "To the capitol at 9 A.M., federal courts at 10, capitol at noon, court in P.M. then to office to write." She had to take a different slant for each paper because readers in New Mexico, Arizona, and California all had different positions on the Boulder Dam bill. Northern and Southern Californians were also split over the benefits of a dam. According to Finney, *Los Angeles Times* publisher Harry Chandler wanted water for Mexico because he had property there. The debates generated "filibusters, letters sent by truckloads and phone calls," she wrote in her autobiography.[42] By the time the final congressional debates on the Swing-Johnson Bill took place, other publications recognized the story as big news and Finney's colleagues viewed her as an expert. "I had to educate the rest of the press corps," she acknowledged proudly.[43]

She remained on the power story even after the Swing-Johnson Bill passed. That same year Montana senator Thomas Walsh called for hearings to investigate the larger issue of private utility company monopolies in electrical power sales and generation. The companies developed pyramid structures that, according to Finney, "created an unnecessary burden on ratepayers." The power industry hearings lasted seven years and unearthed a mountain of information about unethical industry practices. Finally, in 1935, Congress introduced the Public Utility Act. Finney was one of only two reporters who followed the story throughout the entire process. Hearings, she reported, "were held in dingy rooms with whirring fans and clanking radiators." She personally investigated and unearthed political scandals, including the fact that President Herbert Hoover's appointee to a federal power commission had close industry ties. As a result of her stories, the appointment was withdrawn.

She gained access to utility company books, which showed that they had earned astronomical profits by watering stock, transferring ownership, and selling power across state lines.[44]

The power industry stories brought Finney deserved recognition from her employers. In January 1931 Scripps Howard Washington editor Lowell Mellett nominated Finney for a Pulitzer Prize. "I am led to make this nomination not only because of my knowledge of Miss Finney's performance . . . but because I have been urged to do so by a great many members of the profession," he wrote.[45] Senators Hiram Johnson and Thomas Walsh also submitted letters of support to the Pulitzer committee.

Even before the Pulitzer submission, Finney's tenacious work on the power stories had once again made her the subject of newspaper and magazine coverage. The writers seldom failed to note the seeming incongruity of her femininity, modesty, and fearless reporting. In one December 1927 article from a paper called the *Argus*, a writer declared: "It probably is mere coincidence that the best newspaperwoman in Washington is also the most attractive and the most feminine." A story in *The Matrix*, the magazine of a women's press organization, said that Finney, "young, slight, retiring in nature, and of the most distinctly feminine type," has made a name for herself as one of the most fearless and capable reporters in the Capital."[46]

When one interviewer asked Finney to describe her experiences as a female reporter in Washington, she responded with characteristic caution. "Political newspaper work is easier for women in Washington than anywhere else. In covering state legislatures and home politics, most information is obtained in hotel rooms and lobbies or in saloons or elsewhere over a drink." In the nation's capital, however, "the senators and congressmen all have individual offices where it is easy and practicable to interview them. My chief difficulty has been that very often when I interview a man, he takes up a lot of time asking me how I happened to take up this work . . . after getting past that stage, however, I have no more difficulty."[47] Finney's tenacious work on the power story also earned her plaudits from her female colleagues. Bess Furman, who covered Congress for the Associated Press, declared her the only reporter, man or woman, who understood the Boulder Dam project. "I had to go through a book three inches thick to find out what it was all about."[48]

Finney's diary for these years offers private testimony to her pride in her work and her strong interest in peer recognition and respect. She saved letters from prominent people, including Hiram Johnson. In one letter the California senator wrote: "You gave me an entirely new angle on the Sacco case . . . martyrdom, singularly enough is something we can view with a fair degree of philosophy in others, but which we seek to avoid for ourselves."[49] Finney exulted in January 1928 when she "scooped the world on (Hiram) Johnson's resolution calling for investigation of the phone monopoly!"[50]

But her ebullience was sometimes tempered with insecurity, depression, and frustration. When she turned thirty in March 1928, she lamented, "Worse luck. Beyond earning a living I have accomplished little. I have stock and money totaling almost $10,000, but have not written anything worthwhile." And, in June of that year, she was "furious when Cal papers arrived" and the *San Francisco News* had not used her Boulder Dam filibuster story. The next month she again was "furious" when her editor denied her request to be assigned to the Herbert Hoover presidential campaign train. "He said it was a bum assignment for a girl," she wrote angrily.[51]

Her intense focus on her career abated only temporarily when in early 1929 and in the midst of the power industry hearings, Finney married Robert S. Allen, a reporter for the *Christian Science Monitor*. She was nearly thirty-one, and he was two years younger. Although she loved Allen, she was uncertain about marriage up to the actual date of the nuptials. She makes few mentions of Allen in her autobiography, but her diaries contain numerous references to the couple's courtship, to her fears of losing her independence, and to her feelings about being a working wife whose ambition matched that of her husband. Four months before the wedding, in November 1928, she spent all day in hearings on the Swing-Johnson Bill. "Bob irked because no letter from me," she wrote to her diary, "so I sent one off." In January she wrote, "I'm frightened by the prospect of marriage." "Getting a lot of advice." Immediately after the couple married in March 1929 they both went back to work and saved the honeymoon for later.[52]

The marriage was unusual for its time. The couple never had children, and Finney never addressed this issue in either her diary or her autobiography. Publicly she allowed herself to be called Mrs. Robert Allen, but professionally she kept her own name. She insisted on splitting expenses and at one point noted, "Mortgage due. Had to borrow half of it from Bob – $1,840 – to make up $8,000. Won't collect for his half of household expenses until have repaid."[53] And she competed professionally with Allen, at least in her own mind.

Her ego was deflated beginning in 1931, when Allen's career got a significant boost. *Time* magazine identified him along with journalist Drew Pearson as the authors of an anonymous book on Washington politics titled *Washington Merry-Go-Round*. The best-selling book contained unflattering portraits of politicians, including President Herbert Hoover and many of Allen and Pearson's fellow journalists, whom they dubbed sycophantic and ignorant.[54] The book made flattering references to Finney, however.

Allen and Pearson were fired by their respective newspapers after the book's authorship was discovered, but this did not hinder their careers. Instead it made them instant celebrities, and they started a column, also called "Washington Merry-Go-Round" that was soon syndicated nationally. As noted personalities Allen and Pearson received numerous invitations to appear on radio programs and to write other books and magazine articles. Finney was proud of Allen's growing reputation, but it fueled her insecurity as well. While happily noting that her 1931 Pulitzer Prize submission consisted of 171 pages of her stories, she lamented later that same year, "Bob a success, while I am floundering."[55] While her husband's radio stints drew raves, Finney complained of her own, "I am too stiff and therefore unimpressive."[56]

Her resentment grew as Allen became busier and more prominent. Frequently he asked Finney to help him write magazine articles and to deliver them to publishers. She did as he asked but often with irritation. "Bob got radio program in NY and I had to go downtown to read ticker so he wouldn't miss late bulletins," she wrote at one point. At another, "Wrote an article for *Esquire* for Bob who was too busy."[57]

Although she had intentionally distanced herself from feature writing at the beginning of her career, now she lamented her inability to write this kind of story, which was exactly what her husband was good at. "My only success is writing intellectual pieces about politics, etc," she complained.[58] Although most of the couple's reported arguments had to do with career issues, at least one debate had to do with gender. In April 1930 the couple went to a luncheon to honor Ruth Hanna McCormick, a senatorial candidate from Illinois. Allen was cool on McCormick, but Finney described her as "capable and a credit for her sex. The (senators), stodgy old grandfathers, are awfully upset at the prospect of having to associate with a woman on equal terms." They need not have worried. McCormick lost her race.[59]

Finney did not publicly discuss gender as a source of her

insecurities and resentments, but she was keenly aware of this factor and was interested in improving the professional climate for other women. She demonstrated this concern with remarks she made about her involvement in women's press organizations. Finney joined two women's press organizations in the early 1930s: The Women's National Press Club and Theta Sigma Phi. The latter asked her to join, she surmised, because "they admired the way I work – in that it makes it easier for other women to enter the profession." She claimed to have been "bullied" into joining the WNPC, but she took this affiliation seriously as well and hoped to make the organization a public forum for front-page journalists. Evidence for this can be seen from her part in a 1932 dispute between hard-news and feature reporters over the WNPC presidency. "The society editors, publicity women, resent the rest of us who are reporters – [and] wanted to elect their own candidate as WNPC prez."[60]

An Insider in New Deal Washington

Finney achieved professional respect and status during her first decade in Washington, but her real stature came during the twelve years of Franklin Roosevelt's presidency, when she and her husband moved from close observers of power to a position inside the corridors of power. Although she tried to present herself as an objective journalist by writing factual stories without embellishment or editorializing, Finney clearly was a Roosevelt partisan from the beginning. This frequently put her at odds with Scripps Howard executives. According to journalism historians Edwin and Michael Emery and Nancy Roberts, Scripps Howard chairman Roy Howard, a progressive-leaning businessman during the 1920s and a supporter of Franklin Roosevelt in 1932, broke with the president by the mid-1930s. As a result, the papers in the chain became much more conservative.[61]

Finney may have been at odds with her editors, but her

support of Roosevelt put her squarely in the mainstream of Washington reporters, who strongly supported the New Deal. In his 1937 book on Washington correspondents Leo Rosten suggested a motive for this attitude, "Scratch a journalist and you find a reformer," he wrote.[62] This seems an accurate reflection of Finney's sentiments. Throughout her long career, she generally supported progressive causes and could be viewed as a political liberal. But the Allens' enthusiasm, and that of other journalists, also stemmed from the fact that both Franklin and Eleanor Roosevelt understood – much better than their predecessors had – the value of cultivating good relations with the press. From the beginning they courted and flattered political reporters.

During the New Deal years Finney did not abandon her modest and feminine appearance but exhibited even more assertiveness in her approach to her work and to her colleagues. She chose to attend the president's press conferences with men rather than attend Eleanor Roosevelt's press conferences with other women. She proved willing in at least one instance to buck the male press establishment – very publicly – in an effort to get a women's restroom installed near the Senate press gallery. And she reached outside the journalism field for a broader audience, attempting to write screenplays and plays.

Finney became a devotee of Roosevelt before he ran for president. Her early support was based in part on his role in the struggle over the direction of the power industry. She first met the future president in 1931, when he was governor of New York. She visited New York State as part of her coverage of the power industry, to report on Roosevelt's campaign to regulate utilities and to develop a power project on the St. Lawrence River. And she reported on a clash between President Hoover, Roosevelt's soon-to-be presidential rival, and Roosevelt over the St. Lawrence River project. An instant Roosevelt fan, Finney exclaimed to her diary, "What does a president need legs for?"[63]

Finney may have been predisposed toward Roosevelt because of Hoover's role in ferreting out Allen and Pearson as the authors of *Washington Merry Go-Round.* Hoover reportedly asked the Department of Justice to investigate the authorship because of the book's unflattering depictions of him.[64] Finney also was appalled by Hoover's role in routing the Bonus Army of World War I veterans who came to Washington seeking wartime benefits in the summer of 1932. "I stood on the corner of Pennsylvania and 14th to watch," she wrote on August 1. "The White House said Reds controlled the Bonus Army," but they were "well-behaved, desperate men and families."[65]

When Roosevelt won the presidency in November 1932 Finney wrote that she "felt like going around jigging and singing 'Happy Days Are Here Again.'"[66] "I seem to think better of Roosevelt than most of my liberal friends," she wrote.[67] Many years later, explaining her strong support for Roosevelt, Finney said she viewed FDR as "engaged in a desperate struggle to save the free enterprise system" from power politics. And he did save the system, Finney argued.[68]

The first year of the New Deal was a "reporters' paradise," noted Finney. During the administrations of Warren Harding, Calvin Coolidge, and Herbert Hoover, "the Washington press corps had become, for the most part, a bunch of dull-eyed, listless time-servers."[69] But no more. Now a continual flow of stories on New Deal legislation poured from the White House and from Congress. Both Roosevelts held press conferences weekly, as did some cabinet officials, including Secretary of the Interior Harold Ickes. She deemed FDR's press conferences terrific. "You can ask anything you want."[70]

As for Eleanor Roosevelt's press conferences, Finney admitted that they were unprecedented, and she was among the small group of women reporters who helped Eleanor Roosevelt set up her first press conference in March 1933. As media historian Maurine Beasley has noted, Lorena Hickok, Roosevelt's closest confidante, was the catalyst for the Monday morning press briefings. A retired Associated Press reporter who covered Eleanor Roosevelt when she was first lady of New York, Hickok knew the frustrations of being labeled a woman reporter. And she knew that the Depression had made women journalists potentially expendable. Weekly press conferences open only to women journalists would mean more jobs, Hickok told Roosevelt, whose initial briefing took place during her first week in the White House. Roosevelt continued the tradition throughout her tenure as first lady. About thirty-five women usually attended the gatherings.[71] But after the first few press conferences, Finney "left them to specialists in first lady affairs" and began to cover the president's instead.[72]

The National Industrial Recovery Act and the continuing power industry hearings were Finney's primary journalistic beats during the first years of the New Deal. As she had done from the beginning of her career, she exhibited an obsession with not being scooped. She particularly worried about Turner Catledge of the *New York Times*, her primary competitor on the National Recovery Administration (NRA) story. In pursuit of exclusives, "I lost weight and wished I had time to buy a pair of shoes to replace the ones worn out by the peculiar shuffling gait" developed by running down slippery corridors.[73] Her diligence paid off in July 1933. When she spied Catledge standing outside a meeting room where administration officials were discussing the NRA, she took up a post there as well, eating candy bars for dinner. Catledge left the building when the *New York Times* nightly deadline passed, but Finney remained until 11:30 P.M. She was rewarded with an exclusive about the creation of the Blue Eagle program that was designed to encourage business and consumer cooperation in the NRA. Her story put the program into comforting, familiar, gendered terms: "Women, who do most of the country's buying, are asked by President Roosevelt and his Recovery Administration to buy nothing, after August 1, from stores that do not display a government badge showing membership in the National Recovery Administration."[74] To her diary Finney exulted, "Scoop of Turner Catledge on NRA Blue Eagle." And "Washington is the most exciting place in the world just now." Covering the NRA, she added, was "the most fun I've had."[75]

Coverage of the NRA brought her wider public exposure, and in November 1933 Finney was invited to speak on the subject at the Women's Democratic Club. Later that year she began writing a national political column for Scripps Howard to be distributed nationwide. Her growing stature within the journalism community was apparent when in 1934 she was asked to write the essay on front-page reporting for a book on careers for women. Catherine Filene, the *New York Herald-Tribune*'s women's page editor compiled the book.[76] Finney also gained public attention for her work on behalf of the Roosevelt administration, specifically for Hugh Johnson, head of the NRA.

From time to time Finney and Allen wrote speeches for Johnson, an action that seemed to cross the lines between journalism and public relations. It is difficult to know why Finney agreed to be Johnson's speechwriter since she never explained it in her diaries. It seems somewhat out of character because she clearly prized her journalistic integrity. Perhaps the sense of importance overrode any scruples she may have had. Or she may have begun to abandon her heretofore cautious strategy and recognized that she had made it as a reporter and no longer needed to be so careful.

No matter what her motives, throughout the 1930s Finney offered strong opinions on New Deal policies in letters and conversations and wrote about them for Scripps Howard. In January 1937 she told Labor Secretary Frances Perkins she thought FDR's plan to reorganize federal agencies by putting them in the executive branch was "lousy." And she wrote an article for the official inaugural program for Roosevelt's second term, explaining why the date had been moved from March to January.[77]

In May and June 1937 Finney published a series of articles on Eleanor Roosevelt. It said nearly as much about Finney's attitude toward women's rights as it did about the first lady. Roosevelt "called attention to the work of unsung women in various important posts," wrote Finney. "She [broke] precedents and won additional respect for her sex by her personal achievements. She defends the right of women to work outside the home."[78] Finney reflected the same attitude in private musings to herself. In June 1937 she noted in her diary that Congresswoman Mary T. Norton of New Jersey would "be in charge of the wage-hour bill on the house floor – the first woman to pilot a major bill."[79] After interviewing Harriet Elliot, the only woman out of seven Roosevelt appointees chosen to expedite national defense on the eve of World War II, Finney wrote, "Women are always given these impossible chores and are supposed, I guess, to be flattered by the attention."[80]

Three months after the Eleanor Roosevelt series, Scripps Howard editors decided to reassign Finney. Instead of covering the national beat, she now was to focus only on California-related stories from Washington DC. Finney viewed this as a demotion and believed her pro-Roosevelt approach had played a prominent role in the reassignment. "Not happy this year. Papers' anti-New Deal," she wrote. "My services are less and less in demand since everyone understands I won't do jobs I don't believe in. I don't need the job for survival, but I do need it as a way of life."[81]

While Finney was getting less applause from her employers, she was gaining attention from an unlikely source – Hollywood. "For several years before World War II, I lived a delirious double life," Finney wrote in her autobiography. Jacob Wilk, the head of the story department at Warner Brothers, sought her help in writing a script in which Bette Davis would play a newspaper city editor. The film was never made, but Finney did serve as a consultant to director Frank Capra on the 1940 film *Mr. Smith Goes to Washington.*[82] She also wrote plays herself, but they were never produced.

This new outlet may have tempered Finney's depression about her demotion because she never allowed it to dampen her journalistic ambition. She now began to focus on high-profile California stories that she was certain would get national play. She interviewed people such as Harry Bridges, a labor leader, and Tom Mooney, who was pardoned in 1939 after a long jail term for a San Francisco bombing he always maintained he did not commit. She wrote a series of stories on migrant families and their problems in California, a topic that fiction writers such as John Steinbeck and photographers, including Dorothea Lange, were also tackling at this point.

Her stories coincided with congressional hearings into the problems of the unemployed who flooded California because of economic devastation elsewhere in the United States. Some proposed solutions by lawmakers included sending the migrants to Brazil, stopping them at the state's border, and barring migrants from getting any federal relief money until they had been in California five years. Sympathizing with the unemployed, Finney wrote of one case where the brother-in-law of a migrant was tried and convicted for helping his jobless family enter California.[83]

Finney's refusal to do jobs she did not believe in at this point was matched by her growing willingness to confront her colleagues – male and female – on gender issues she saw as important. Her continuing obsession with being taken seriously led her to propose in March 1934 that the Women's National Press Club limit itself to hard-news reporters. This proposal "set off a near-riot from the publicity clique," she wrote in her diary.[84] The press club continued to include publicity women, despite her efforts.

Another campaign involved male colleagues and her effort to convince them to have a restroom installed on the gallery floor for women reporters covering Congress. Until 1937 women reporters had to walk down two floors from the press gallery to use the tourists' restroom, while male reporters had a restroom of their own on the gallery floor. Previous efforts to get a restroom installed met with resistance, both from members of Congress and from male colleagues. In 1936 the women sought permission to get an empty room converted to a bathroom, but their male colleagues claimed they needed the space for file cabinets.

Finney did not believe this story and, after waiting several months for her chance, she obtained a key to the room and found that no file cabinets had been installed. Outraged, she went over her male colleagues' heads to Congress. Testifying before the House Appropriations Committee, she sought funds for a women's restroom. In January 1937 Finney and eight other women reporters finally christened the new bathroom near the Senate press gallery. "We rigged up a fancy centerpiece with lavender toilet paper and toy bathroom fixtures," she explained.[85]

World War II and Beyond

By the early 1940s Finney was back in favor at Scripps Howard and was writing on national rather than regional issues. She covered the Dies Committee, the forerunner of the House Committee on Un-American Activities that investigated "radicals." She wrote about the Selective Service Act, enacted in expectation of World War II, and how former California senator William McAdoo enlisted at the age of 76. She covered the United States Supreme Court and the debates on continuing United States neutrality in the face of growing threats from Germany and Japan. By this point she had distanced herself from her old friend Hiram Johnson by declaring him "unbalanced and an appeaser."[86]

Her renewed stature was distinguished in a new, nationally syndicated column, "Washington Calling," that she began writing in 1941. She offered readers her views on politics, economic forecasts, and her analysis of national and world events. Finney also frequently wrote for other publications. "Got $125 from *American Mercury* for story about interstate trade barriers," she wrote in her diary in March 1940. In early December 1941, just before the bombing of Pearl Harbor, she came up with the idea of another column called "In the Offing." It contained news that Finney compiled and wrote from Scripps Howard national and foreign staffs.

From about 1939 on her diary contains few references to gender and much less comment about perceived slights and inequities. She no longer discussed women's "firsts" and seemed less competitive about her husband's success. "Bob and Drew on radio program Sunday at 7:30," she wrote in her diary in 1940, "there go our Sundays."[87] But she still exhibited occasionally shaky self-confidence despite all of her accomplishments. When the Scripps Howard paper in Denver canceled her column in the summer of 1941, she wrote in her diary, "They don't consider me worth the contribution they have been making to my salary."[88] Other papers made up the salary, however, and she did not lose any money.

This diminishing emphasis on gender might be attributed to the fact that women were filling more and more nontraditional jobs by 1940 as the war approached, and that many of the professional battles had been won. But the coming war itself was more likely the cause. Her diary was filled with items on the pending conflict. In May 1941 Finney fumed about Charles Lindbergh's declaration that the country should turn to new leadership, away from FDR – "it sounds like sedition to me." And just before Pearl Harbor she wrote, "Wrought up about war, job, making blackout curtains. No place safe."[89]

Her fear largely stemmed from her husband's insistence on enlisting despite the fact that he was over forty. In July 1942 Allen reported for duty. Just after he left Finney noted wryly to her diary that the last few days the couple spent together represented "the first time in our married life that he has been home to eat dinner with me, except on vacation."[90] After he left he sent her a telegram declaring her to be "the bravest, truest wife any man ever had."[91] Finney ended her diary just after Allen left for war.

During the war Finney continued writing about politics. Her prominence can be seen by her invitation in 1942, along with thirteen other well-known women reporters, to tour defense plants across the country. The women were feted by government officials who accompanied them to the various sites. Newspapers across the country carried photos of them on tours and having meals in the plants. Much of the coverage featured women defense workers who filled in for men away at war. From Seattle Finney wrote, "In the Pacific Northwest, manpower is becoming womanpower so fast you can almost see it happen." One executive told her, she wrote, that "in operations requiring deftness, (women) are better than men. But they have higher absentee rates." She attributed this to the lack of childcare. In Portland, Oregon, Finney wrote of women hired to work in sawmills and shipyards who were "proud of broken fingernails." And in Los Angeles, she declared that "the battle of production may be won or lost in the end by women," who were "less likely to fumble rivets and more nimble."[92]

Finney's career in many ways was bracketed by the two world wars. She entered the profession in the midst of World War I as men left home to fight in Europe, gained prominence and stature in the 1920s and 1930s, and by

World War II clearly was considered one of the top women in her field. It is impossible to know how she saw her own success at this point, and whether she believed she had lived up to the ambitions she articulated in her youth.

World War II also made Finney the primary breadwinner. Wounded in Germany in 1945, Allen lost an arm below the elbow. Although he continued working as a journalist after the war, he never regained the prominence he had enjoyed before the war. This had to do with his relationship with Drew Pearson as well as with his injuries. Before enlisting Allen arranged for Pearson to pay Finney a percentage of Allen's income from *Washington Merry-Go-Round*. Pearson failed to do so and the two men had a permanent falling out.

Finney, meanwhile, kept working, writing stories and her political column until she retired in the mid-1960s. But she began to slow down somewhat by the 1950s and early 1960s. Because she stopped writing in her diary in 1942, because her autobiography relied so heavily on diary references, and because her stories and columns rarely, if ever, dealt with gender at this point, it is difficult to discern what Finney thought about the subject at the end of her career. Articles she cut out of newspapers provide the only clues to her sentiments. One such article was the obituary of French restaurateur Jean-Baptiste Troisgros, in which the writer quoted Troisgros: "You must treat the woman gently, but you mustn't be frightened. . . . From 35 to 45 women are old and at 45, the devil takes over and they're beautiful, splendid, maternal and proud. . . . They are worth going out to find, and because of them some men never grow old."[93]

But others did take note of her significance. At a 1947 dinner a speaker called her the "leading woman political writer in Washington." "She is the only woman in the country to write lead political stories for a national string of papers."[94] In the 1950s, discussing Finney's work as a columnist covering quadrennial political party conventions,

Scripps Howard managing editor Dick Thornburg noted, "Ruth fails to give herself anything like the amount of credit she deserves" for her success.[95] And a photo of Finney sitting at her desk in the early 1960s carried the inscription in one corner, "the best rewriteman in the office."[96]

One of the most telling reflections of how Finney's colleagues saw her came after her death in March 1979 in an obituary her husband cut out and kept with her personal papers. Writer Irving Leibowitz described how much he owed to Finney's guidance during his early days as a reporter when she shepherded him through the pitfalls of political news coverage. His description would undoubtedly have pleased her: "She was a career woman who was secure in her own abilities. . . . As a journalist, she discovered you could crusade just by telling the truth. As a person, she unselfishly touched many lives." But most important, added Leibowitz, "she made her life count for something."[97]

Charlotta Bass in the newsroom of
her weekly paper, the *California Eagle*,
1930s. As publisher and editor of the
Eagle from 1912 to 1951, Bass helped to
formulate and implement strategies
for confronting oppression and discrimination. Courtesy of the *California Eagle* and the Charlotta Bass Collections, Southern California Library
for Social Studies and Research.

3. The Press As Pulpit

Charlotta Bass and the California Eagle

In 1960, as she looked back at her forty-year career as a journalist, Charlotta Bass wrote of her belief that "the press and
pulpit serve as the two main centers for developing community consciousness."[1] She was speaking of the African American community, which had used the black press as a forum
for protest and uplift since before the Civil War.[2] From 1912
to 1951 Bass herself played a dominant role in this commu-
nity-building process. As publisher and editor of the weekly
African American newspaper, the *California Eagle*, based in
Los Angeles, she reflected and also helped shape debates
about race and power, both in California and in the country
at large.

In some ways Bass resembled other African American
publishers: T. Thomas Fortune of the *New York Age*, Robert
Abbott of the *Chicago Defender*, and Robert Vann of the *Pitts-
burgh Courier*. All played prominent roles in the national
fight against discrimination and oppression. In other important ways, however, Bass differed from them. Her paper
was smaller, with a circulation of less than 10,000, compared
to the *Defender*, for example, which had a circulation of more
than 100,000. She was a woman, an anomaly in a job domi-
nated by men, both black and white, throughout most of
American history.

Bass also stood in a unique position with regard to other
women journalists, both black and white. As a publisher she
held more power within the black community than did
other female African American journalists. She did not have
to convince male employers to hire her or allow her to write

front-page news. But like other black female journalists, she had to work within a framework that embraced traditional female roles as a way of building the self-esteem of black men. This same framework governed the careers of white women, and, like them, Bass had to use her pulpit creatively and cautiously to gain acceptance from men. But Bass was much more of an insider in political and cultural debates than white women. As publisher of Los Angeles's longest-lasting African American paper until 1933, when another successful paper, the *Sentinel*, appeared, she helped to formulate and implement strategies for confronting oppression and discrimination.

Bass's unusual circumstances enabled her to cross many barriers, race- and gender-based. She focused most of her energy, at least overtly, on race issues – police brutality, employment discrimination by government agencies and private businesses, negative stereotyping of African Americans, and lynching. But between the lines she also took on gender stereotypes. She did this by personal example, through columns and stories depicting women as strong and achieving, and by putting other women into prominent positions on the *Eagle*.

In her dual role as advocate for African Americans and for women, Bass's experiences reflect the intersection between race and gender discussed in the works of many prominent historians who have examined this nexus. These scholars have concluded that the unique niche they occupy has enabled black women to see the crucial connection between race and gender more clearly than most white women. While bell hooks [*sic*] argues that black women, given the choice of fighting for race or gender equality, have generally chosen race – frequently to their detriment – others see the choices somewhat differently.[3]

Paula Giddings views black women as the "linchpin between the struggle for black rights and women's rights." As such they "loosened the chains around both" groups, she argues, understanding that women's rights represented an "empty promise if blacks remained crushed under a racist power structure."[4] As Patricia Hill Collins argued, the pivotal roles historically played by black women in forging community resistance against oppression has made them a powerful force in that community. The struggle against both racism and sexism stimulated independence and self-reliance in black women, declares Collins. She concedes that black men, like their white "brothers," have perpetuated gender stereotypes as well. But because in black culture both men and women historically have participated in the public sphere, many black women have frequently managed to resist this stereotype.[5]

The African American newspaper represented one significant venue for this resistance. In choosing journalism as her public platform, Bass joined a long line of black women journalists extending back into the early nineteenth century. They included Mary Ann Shadd, who promoted abolition and women's suffrage in the antebellum period; Fannie Williams, a journalist and founder of the National Association of Colored Women (NACW) who urged black women to organize and focus attention on the double bind of race and sex; and Gertrude Mossell, who promoted women's rights, suffrage, and social reform in the postbellum period.[6]

But the anti-lynching crusader Ida B. Wells was the journalist with whom Bass most clearly identified. Born a slave in Mississippi during the Civil War, Wells began her journalism career by writing in black newspapers about her unsuccessful 1884 lawsuit against the Chesapeake and Ohio Railroad, which had ejected her from a seat in the white section of the train. By the late 1880s, using the pen name Iola, she wrote for several African American newspapers, and in 1889 she bought a one-third interest in the *Memphis Free Speech and Headlight*. In 1891 T. Thomas Fortune, publisher of the *New York Age*, said of her, "If Iola were a man she would be a humming independent in politics. She has plenty of nerve and is as sharp as a steel trap."[7]

It was in the 1890s that Wells earned her reputation as a fearless advocate to stop lynching. She was willing, at every juncture, to incur the wrath of racist white Southerners by openly contradicting their assertion that the rape of white women by black men was the motive for lynching. She urged blacks to boycott white businesses and to relocate to less hostile territory in the Southwest.[8]

Bass, like Wells, proved willing, on dozens of occasions, to put herself in harm's way in pursuit of racial justice. Like Wells she sometimes proved so uncompromising that she made other African Americans uncomfortable.[9] Both women tried to prevent the release of the racist 1915 film *Birth of A Nation* and fought the Ku Klux Klan through the 1920s. In the 1930s after Wells died, Bass challenged discrimination by the federal government in Depression relief efforts and by the Federal Bureau of Investigation during World War II. Bass refused to stop criticizing the government's racial policies in the face of threats to revoke her mailing privileges. She used the *California Eagle* to encourage African Americans to stand up against oppression by lobbying government officials, boycotting white establishments, and protesting blacks' exclusion from jobs such as streetcar conductors, nurses, and telephone operators. She publicly denounced such racist practices as restrictive covenants – contractual agreements that kept blacks out of white neighborhoods.

Although race issues trumped gender debates for Wells and Bass, both women also used their experiences to suggest the possibilities for women in the professional and political spheres. Wells helped to found the National Association for the Advancement of Colored People (NAACP), the Negro Fellowship League, and the Equal Rights League. Bass participated in the NAACP and briefly held a local office in Marcus Garvey's United Negro Improvement Association (UNIA). She helped to found both the Industrial Council, a Los Angeles organization aimed at protesting unjust hiring practices, and the Home Owners' Protective Association, to lobby against restrictive covenants.

Both women used networks of female activists to further their causes and publicize women's achievements. In her autobiography Wells noted with pride her affiliation with the National Association of Colored Women, strong supporters of her anti-lynching campaign, and her association with successful businesswomen such as Madam C. J. Walker, founder and director of a cosmetics empire. "I was very proud of her success," wrote Wells, "because I had met Madam Walker when she first started out eleven years before. . . . To see her phenomenal rise made me take pride anew in Negro womanhood."[10]

In the columns of her newspaper Bass promoted women and their achievements. In her self-published autobiography, she listed women who were pioneers in Los Angeles and in their professional fields. She included Biddy Mason, a slave who fought for her freedom in California and worked her way into wealth as a Los Angeles realtor in the nineteenth century; Beatrice Owen, the first black woman to fly across the continent; and Virginia Stephens, the first black woman to pass the California state bar examination.[11] She promoted women who ran for political office – even white ones like Estelle Lawton Lindsay, who was elected to the Los Angeles City Council in 1917. "Her victory and her performance in office were significant for they revealed (1) that . . . women could be elected to office, and (2) that once elected, they could help create good government," Bass wrote.[12]

Finally, neither Wells nor Bass was modest at all. Both wrote autobiographies promoting themselves along with the causes they undertook, although neither saw her autobiography published in her lifetime. Bass used the pages of the *Eagle* to tout her persuasive abilities and her prominence. A 1930 article described a Bass speech in which she urged her listeners not to reelect Governor James Rolph. "Mrs. Bass spoke and convinced. She argued, she extolled, she won vote upon vote," the reporter noted enthusiastically.[13]

Like many white women journalists in the interwar period, Bass was married, and she offered readers of her newspaper the vision of an equal partnership, rather than a traditional marriage. She married rather late in life, when she was around forty, and her husband, Joseph Bass, also published the *Eagle*. He worked as editor while she took the title managing editor. Technically his was the higher position, but Charlotta Bass maintained a comparable community profile to that of her husband. Although she clearly respected Joseph Bass, who had a lengthy career in African American journalism before he came to Los Angeles, she stood on her own. The couple never had children, and she never publicly discussed her childlessness. But it enabled her to travel throughout the country, attend meetings, give speeches, and visit other African American newspapers.

It might be argued that Bass's prominence was limited to the black community, which would mitigate her influence as a role model for the larger audience that watched white front-page women breaking barriers throughout the 1920s to 1940s, but this is not an accurate perception. Because she combined journalism and political activism, her influence extended into the white community as well. She was active in the Republican Party before switching to the Progressive Party in the late 1940s, and she appeared before the Los Angeles City Council and County Board of Supervisors on numerous occasions, seeking jobs and services for African Americans. She served as the first black member of the Los Angeles Grand Jury in 1943. She ran, unsuccessfully, for City Council in 1945 and for vice president on the left-leaning Independent Progressive Party ticket in 1952.

It might also be argued that Bass was too radical to represent the cautious brand of protofeminism reflected in the lives of white female journalists in this period. In fact she did grow to be quite radical by the late 1940s and challenged not only racial oppression but also the exclusion of poor people of all ethnic groups from the American dream. Although she was never a Communist, by the early 1950s she espoused a coalition of working class people of all races and both genders. But Bass came to this radicalism slowly.

And in her shifting political sentiments, Bass's experiences mirrored those of some other prominent African Americans who either flirted with leftist politics or became dedicated radicals by the ends of their lives: W. E. B. DuBois, writer and musician James Weldon Johnson, writer Richard Wright, and actor Paul Robeson. Her contemporary Marvel Cooke even joined the Communist Party in the 1930s. Like many others Bass came to her radicalism over a long lifetime of deep disappointment and disillusionment with efforts to force whites to treat African Americans with respect.[14]

Until the late 1940s Bass remained firmly within the mainstream of African American political thought. She promoted uplift and self-help in the 1920s, a decade in which black leaders and journalists "shared the idea that bourgeois achievement was a prerequisite for black liberation," according to Judith Stein.[15] By the 1930s many black newspapers had shifted their emphasis away from uplift and toward gaining employment and fighting discrimination on public relief projects. Bass helped to promote the nationwide "Don't Buy Where You Can't Work" campaign, an economic strategy aimed at welding community solidarity to protest unfair hiring practices. And during World War II she participated enthusiastically in the "Double V for Victory" program, an effort by the black press to link the fight against fascism abroad to the struggle against racism at home.

Although her approach to racial issues changed over time, the same cannot be said for gender. Throughout her long career Bass never wavered in her efforts to demonstrate that women might be different from men, but that this did not mean they were not equal as well. The vision she promoted and the community she helped to nurture was, in large part, based on her crusades for women as well as for African Americans.

Bass's Road to Front-Page Journalism

Little is known about Charlotta Bass before she came to Los Angeles in 1910, and she seems to have wanted it that way. Although she made references in her autobiography to a life on the East Coast, the details are sketchy. She said she was born in Little Compton, Rhode Island, but never mentioned a birth year. Other sources offer varying birth dates, ranging from 1890 – in a campaign biography when she ran for vice president – to 1874, which was the date on her 1969 death certificate filed in Los Angeles County. Reference books cite an 1880 birth date. Sources also offer different birthplaces. Her death certificate notes that she was born in Ohio but reference books place her birthplace in South Carolina. Bass also claimed four siblings – two brothers and two sisters – in her autobiography, but other sources claim she was one of eleven children. Sources also give her maiden name as Spears, but it occasionally appeared on her newspaper masthead as Spear.[16] Bass did say she came to Los Angeles from Providence, Rhode Island, for health reasons. Whatever her background she was following the path trod by thousands of others, of all ethnic groups, who came to California to reinvent themselves, and she succeeded in doing so.

When Charlotta Spears arrived in Los Angeles she was either in her twenties or her thirties. From the little she divulged about her background it seems clear that her roots lay in the middle class and that she had some experience being in an integrated society. An undated photo with no location cited shows her sitting in the center of what looks to be a class of high school students. She is well-dressed, but most importantly perhaps, she is one of only five African Americans in a group of nearly fifty.[17] Bass had a large vocabulary and used somewhat flowery language in her writing. She cited books she had read in her youth, including Edward Bellamy's *Looking Backward*, a novel that offered a utopian vision of America at the dawn of the twenty-first century. She frequently wrote about her family, often in conjunction with visits. The suggestion of her class background can be seen in the kinds of social events in which family members participated – club meetings, parties, and theater outings.

Describing her motivation for coming to California, Bass hinted at a relatively privileged upbringing. "A physician had advised me to spend as much time as possible in the sunshine," Bass wrote in her autobiography. "But after a few months, due to the high cost of living, I found it necessary to come out of the sunshine and earn at least a part of my expenses." Since she had worked previously as an "office girl and solicitor" for the *Providence Watchman*, "I took a job collecting and soliciting subscriptions for the *Eagle*," at five dollars a week.[18]

The *Eagle*, founded by transplanted easterner John Neimore in 1879, was the oldest African American newspaper in the West. Nearly a dozen other black publications were published in Los Angeles during Bass's forty-year tenure at the *Eagle*. Most lasted only a year or two. The two main exceptions were the *Tribune* and the *Sentinel*; the former started publishing in 1940 and the latter in 1933.[19] Bass compared her paper to the Underground Railroad, a vast network of safe houses in the antebellum South that were used to guide slaves to freedom in the North. Neimore saw the *Eagle*, according to Bass, as "an agency to attract Negroes to California, where they would enjoy a greater portion of freedom and human rights than in their former slave environs."[20]

When Bass arrived at the *Eagle*, however, the paper was having financial difficulties, Neimore was in poor health, and Los Angeles was being rapidly transformed from the welcoming place Neimore had envisioned to a racist environment. As more people – both African Americans fleeing the South and white Protestants from the Midwest – arrived in the city in the early twentieth century, town leaders began recreating the same segregated and oppressive conditions that existed elsewhere. African Americans remained a small segment of the overall population, but their numbers grew along with those of other groups during the period from 1910 to 1950. By 1910 Los Angeles had a population of about 300,000, with about 7,600 blacks. Twenty years later 1,238,000 people lived in Los Angeles and nearly 39,000 of them were black. By 1940 the city had 1.5 million residents of whom nearly 64,000 were black.[21]

Starting around 1910 blacks, along with other non-Anglo ethnic groups including Asian Americans and Mexican Americans, were pushed out of white neighborhoods and into the southern and eastern parts of the city. Restrictive covenants were created to keep minorities out of white neighborhoods. And whites tried to keep blacks from gaining political power. In the 1920s when large numbers of blacks moved into Watts, a railroad town south of Los Angeles, the Los Angeles City Council voted to incorporate it to prevent black self-government.[22]

No Jim Crow laws existed in California, but African Americans had difficulty obtaining work in white-dominated industries or in civil service jobs. Most remained clustered at or near the bottom of the economic scale, working on farms or as domestics. By the late 1910s, however, a small black business class had developed. Lawyers, doctors, dentists, ministers, real estate brokers, and insurance company owners represented the largest occupational categories throughout the first half of the twentieth century. Blacks also worked as barbers, manufacturers, builders, and retailers.[23]

This small business class represented the advertising base and intended readership of the *California Eagle*. However the growing racial antagonism in Los Angeles led the newspaper to focus both on society events and stories designed to appeal to middle-class readers and on efforts to combat discrimination and oppression from hostile white officials. The paper also discussed racial issues of national import: lynching, segregation, and the competing agendas of national black leaders. When Bass arrived in California, the *Eagle* was a mixed-up jumble of stories and advertisements. Each page carried as many as fifteen to twenty stories, and it was difficult to tell where one story ended and another began.

Shortly after her arrival, according to Bass, Neimore undertook a trip to restore his failing health and "the responsibility of getting the *Eagle* to press and off the press became the lot of the newly hired, yet highly inspired young woman who was destined to occupy a peculiar place in the realm of newspaper publishing."[24] Neimore did not recover and, in February 1912, on his deathbed, he asked Bass to take over operation of the newspaper. Reluctantly, she agreed. It was the beginning of a career that would test and shape her in ways she never could have imagined. The paper had $10 in assets and $150 in debts when it became Bass's. For months she saved money by eating a diet consisting primarily of crackers and milk.[25]

In telling the story of how she came to publish the *Eagle*, Bass presented her gender as a significant issue. The way she depicted herself in her autobiography, she seemed interested in having prominent black leaders view her as nonthreatening yet devoted to her job and competent to handle any situation, similar to strategies employed by white female journalists. She made it clear that she faced some challenges because of her sex. "Who ever heard of a woman running a newspaper? It was the talk of the town," she recalled.

She described one conversation she overheard in a cafe between two female *Eagle* readers. "'What about that young girl who came here recently and worked for Mr. Neimore?'" she quoted one young woman asking the other. "'Nobody seems to know her, and they say she will not be able to go it alone,'" the other replied. Male leaders of African American churches in Los Angeles also evinced skepticism over whether a woman could manage such a challenging enterprise, although they lent Bass their printing equipment in exchange for free advertising.[26]

The skepticism also extended to the man who joined Bass in publishing the *Eagle* in 1913. Joseph Bass was fifty years old and a veteran of the African American newspaper business when he arrived in Los Angeles from Topeka, Kansas, where he had worked as a journalist in the 1890s.[27] After visiting several papers, he settled in at the *Eagle*, where he became editor. Reminiscing in the 1930s about his early days on the paper, Joseph Bass recollected that he initially had been leery of the "feminine journalist" who owned the paper. But she quickly won him over:

I had been told that a young woman was the head of this particular newspaper and on that account I had been shy to some extent, or in all possibility, in calling, I had my doubts.... However, after my call and a general shop talk with Miss Charlotta Spear, I was forced to alter my opinion, because it seemed she had every requisite which it takes to be a top-notcher.[28]

Within several months of Joseph Bass's arrival, the business partnership became a life partnership and the couple married. Business still came first, however. "The new combination of editor and managing editor realized that there was no time for romancing," wrote Charlotta Bass, "with the ever-growing (Los Angeles) population which was now definitely heterogeneous and fraught with new problems."[29] Whatever else it brought her, Bass's marriage brought her legitimacy as a female publisher. Because her husband clearly approved of her journalistic activities and, in fact, mostly worked on the financial side of the paper, she was able to write most of the copy and no longer had to confront male skepticism and antagonism about her high profile and professional activities.[30]

The beginning of Joseph Bass's tenure at the *Eagle* coincided with a shift toward a more political orientation. Although the paper continued to carry "social news to please the people who wanted it" as well as church and community events, it also aimed to carry "important issues of the day for those more patriotically inclined."[31] Along with other African American papers, the *California Eagle* joined the effort to stop production of *Birth of a Nation*, D. W. Griffith's 1915 film that glorified the Ku Klux Klan. The film was being made in Los Angeles and was using African American actors. Bass used the pages of the paper to urge them not to work as extras, but the money they earned made her effort difficult. "We did not succeed in stopping production, but we did achieve some small progress by forcing Griffith to cut some of the most vicious attacks against the morals of the Negro people," Bass wrote.[32]

During these early days, Charlotta Bass began to try to build the *Eagle*'s reputation and circulation by traveling throughout California and the West. During one six-week trip through California's Central Valley in 1914, her "political development began in earnest," she noted, as she met with residents of black rural communities who lacked even the most basic amenities. Before this experience Bass's "political understanding was somewhat limited," she acknowledged.[33]

Part of her career strategy seems to have focused on encouraging as many people as possible to see her as a public presence. In 1917 she traveled to Houston, Texas, after a race riot between African American soldiers stationed in Texas and white residents. She walked the streets unaccompanied and undeterred by threats of violence. The editor of a black newspaper in Houston "seemed surprised at seeing me," she noted in her autobiography. "At that time, newspaper women, especially Negro newspaper women, were not seen floating around pushing pencils as freely as now." Other women clearly saw Bass as a role model. In her 1919 history on African Americans in California, Delilah Beasley, a black journalist based in Oakland, concluded that Bass's professional success "inspired others." Friends had worried that she might quit her job after marriage and were pleased when she continued to work as hard as ever.[34] Bass also demonstrated her independence by keeping her own name, using it in conjunction with her married name until at least the mid-1920s.[35]

Women were among the first beneficiaries of Bass's burgeoning political activism. During a 1918 tour of Los Angeles County Hospital, Bass discovered that the facility had no black nurses or nurse's aides. She set up an employment bureau of sorts and then gained backing from the County Board of Supervisors to try to place her clients in jobs, first as aides, then if it worked out, as nurses. She also fought, early in the 1920s, to increase access by African American women to civil service jobs.[36]

By the 1920s when the more assertive "New Negro" began confronting the racist white establishment, Bass was gaining public prominence as an active participant in African American political organizations. She joined the Urban League and played an active role in the Los Angeles chapter of the NAACP, the country's third-largest branch. For a brief time in 1921, she served as co-chair of the Los Angeles branch of Marcus Garvey's United Negro Improvement Association. This may have seemed contradictory because the NAACP and UNIA had such disparate goals – the NAACP's to end segregation and the UNIA's to foster black separatism and independence – but both sought to promote race pride. Despite her role in UNIA Bass promoted integration, not separatism. "The color line is one upon which politicians fatten," a 1922 *Eagle* editorial declared. African Americans could only gain "through alliances with right-thinking" whites.[37] By 1922 Bass and the other Los Angeles leaders had abandoned Garvey as questions began to be raised about his finances and business operations.[38]

Bass participated in national organizations, but most of her efforts were aimed at problems that existed in Los Angeles, and she directly challenged the most fearsome and racist group in existence: the Ku Klux Klan. She protested to the police chief and the city council when Klan members painted KKK graffiti over signs in town and when the Klan tried to burn black families out of their homes. In 1925, she obtained and published a letter by the Klan's California leader G. W. Price; in it he discussed ways to get rid of the three most prominent black leaders from Watts. The letter read, in part: "The best way to get rid of our antagonists is to make them leave Watts in disgrace. . . . The white people of Watts are tired of being run by people who are not 100% Americans." Price suggested planting "a bottle of booze in the enemy's car and hav[ing] enough of the faithful on hand to get a conviction."[39] The Klan sued Bass for libel and declared the letter to be a fake. White newspapers, including the *Los Angeles Times*, covered the ensuing libel trial, at which she was acquitted.

Klan members tried to intimidate Bass out of continuing her crusade against the organization. Using the third person to describe herself, she recalled one experience: "One night when that 'nigger woman' as the KKK described her, was standing alone in a shop, about 50 x 150 feet in size, exposed to the public gaze through a full-size plate glass window, eight of the hooded boys shed their disguise, pulled at the door knob and demanded that they be admitted." Bass remembered that she had a gun in her desk and pulled it out. "This was really a joke," Bass wrote in her autobiography, "she had never handled a gun before and wasn't quite sure which end to point at the intruders." The Klan members did not know this, however, and "beat a hasty retreat."[40] This fearless stance led to Bass's husband reportedly telling her, "Mrs. Bass, one of these days you're going to get me killed." She reportedly replied, "Mr. Bass, it will be in a good cause."[41]

Charlotta Bass As a Front-Page Journalist

By the mid-1920s Bass was well known in Los Angeles political circles and had gained a reputation as a courageous fighter for social and economic justice. But she did not yet have an individual presence or a byline with which a larger audience of readers could identify. This started to change by the later years of the 1920s and early years of the 1930s as she began to find her voice and her identity as a front-page columnist in the *Eagle*. As editor, Joseph Bass undoubtedly played a strong role in guiding editorial policy. He was a prominent leader of the African American community in Los Angeles as well. For example, he helped to found and operate the Industrial Council, an organization created in 1930 to combat discrimination against African Americans by white employers. And the *Eagle* was a staunch promoter of the national "Don't Buy Where You Can't Work" program led by larger black papers. Each week the paper carried a list of businesses where blacks were urged to shop. It urged a boycott of businesses not on the list.

But it was Charlotta Bass who readers saw on the paper's pages, as author of a weekly column called "On the Sidewalk." She exhorted readers to take pride in their ethnicity, railed against city officials who continued to discriminate and oppress African Americans, and discussed larger political and social issues related to race. The paper as a whole began to shift to a more confrontational stance at this time as the Depression took root, and it became clear that the white establishment had to be compelled through government action to provide any help to economically devastated African Americans.

By the mid-1930s the *Eagle* had competition from another significant black paper in Los Angeles, the *Sentinel*, which had a similar approach toward news but less aggressive editors.[42] Unlike white papers that engaged in fierce and sometimes underhanded competition for readers and advertisers, the two African American papers in Los Angeles engaged in a generally friendly rivalry. Many of the staff members of the *Sentinel* received their journalistic training from Bass. In fact, according to Virginia Ann Prince, who wrote a 1946 master's thesis on black newspapers in Los Angeles, "very few outstanding journalists . . . did not at one time or another work with the California *Eagle*." Loren Miller wrote stories and columns for the *Eagle* in the 1930s before he left the paper to work for the *Sentinel*. He eventually became a noted civil rights lawyer and municipal court judge. In 1951 he bought the *Eagle* from Bass. Leon Washington worked for the *Eagle* as an advertising manager before becoming publisher of the *Sentinel*. He worked with Bass on the "Don't Buy Where You Can't Work" program. And no publisher or editor of the *Sentinel* ever had as strong a public presence in Los Angeles as Charlotta Bass during her forty-year tenure.[43]

After Joseph Bass's death in 1934, Charlotta Bass ran the paper alone. By this time she had carved out a prominent role for herself in the African American community at large. As a widow, she also enjoyed respect and deference. She occasionally used the pages of the *Eagle* to offer tribute to her late husband, but Bass seemed to thrive in her solo status. She traveled, made numerous speeches and public appearances, had her picture taken, and promoted her activities in the pages of her newspaper. She also became more aggressive in her demands for economic and political justice for African American citizens of Los Angeles and the United States.

This aggressive position might have been somewhat muted by the appearance of the paper, particularly until the late 1930s. Its front page combined features on visiting residents, laudatory stories about advertisers, hard-hitting news items, and Bass's column. Inside pages also offered an eclectic combination of articles – for example, a 1933 series detailing how the federal government discriminated against African Americans on relief projects ran side by side with church news.

Nonetheless by the late 1920s and early 1930s the paper was much easier to read and had lost its haphazard approach to graphics. On the masthead it was called the "Soaring Eagle," symbolizing the exalted mission the publishers envisioned. Between eight and ten stories appeared on the front page and readers could easily follow a single story from beginning to end, although the line between advertising and editorial content still was not always clear. Mortuaries, life insurance companies, and other African American–owned businesses were the primary advertisers, along with purveyors of beauty products, including hair-straighteners and skin lighteners. The paper claimed a circulation of between 5,000 and 10,000, ranged from twelve to twenty pages, and sold for a nickel.

Bass's first "On the Sidewalk" column appeared in the late 1920s, and she continued to write it until she sold the paper in 1951. Reading the columns it appears that it took Bass at least a year to gain the confidence necessary to tackle, head on, the most pressing issues of concern to African Americans. Her first columns, although designed to foster a sense of community among her readers, were more tentative than those appearing only a few years later. For example, an early column, from 1930, read: "How many of us at the close of each day can consistently check on our thoughts and words to the extent that we may stretch out on our beds and see them pass before our closed eyes, knowing that this day we have done unto our brother even as we would that should do unto us."[44]

A year later her tone was slightly more hard edged. She lamented: "It is sad but true that the Negro has thrown off more easily all of the other disadvantages accumulated in his period of bondage than the lack of confidence in his Black brother."[45]

By 1933, however, she was tackling economic and political issues much more directly: "Americans who read history without race or color prejudice in their minds realize that the Negro American is entitled to a greater opportunity to make a decent living wage than most other Americans – Why? Because first of all he spent about two hundred and fifty years in the debasing school of slavery, during which time he was denied proper food and shelter for full and complete physical and mental development."[46]

She also tackled issues of national significance, such as the Scottsboro case, in which nine young African American men were convicted of raping two white women aboard an Alabama train in 1931. Despite the lack of evidence and the recanted stories of one of the women, the men were given lengthy jail sentences. The Communist Party took the lead in protesting the case, to the embarrassment of African American groups, like the NAACP. Ultimately, the case became a cause célèbre among black and civil rights organizations and many liberals. Bass wrote columns about the case, in which she also asked for black Los Angeles residents to donate money for an appeal. In one column she wrote: "I have read the lines and between the lines, and the only thing I can see is that . . . some colored boys and some white boys and two white women, all poor and all ignorant and illiterate, while tramping from one place to another in search of better food and shelter, met in a gondola car. There was a scramble as to who should ride and who should not. In the battle, the whites were worsted and thrown off the car."[47] After the column ran the black community in Los Angeles created a Citizens Committee for the Defense of the Scottsboro Boys and held a mass meeting and march through the eastside of town.[48]

Bass even took on issues of international import. In 1938 she discussed the growing sentiment for independence among Africans living on the African continent: "The spark of revolution, perhaps not to burst into flame for a quarter or half century, grows brighter weekly in the lands where two hundred thousand whites control over 200 million natives."[49]

Bass's voice and presence was strongest, however, when she sought to personally shape political and economic policies for African Americans in Los Angeles. During the three-year period from 1933 to 1936 she used her column to rail against businesses, such as the Southern California Telephone Company, which eagerly took money from black residents but refused to hire them for even the most menial jobs. Unemployment was a pressing concern for most people during the Depression but particularly for minorities. By 1933 30 percent of black residents in Los Angeles depended on relief payments comparable to figures in the rest of the country.[50]

In May 1933 "On the Sidewalk" promoted an upcoming forum to discuss the issue of employment at the phone company, which received an estimated $720,000 annually from black customers.[51] The following month, Bass's column began raising the possibility that customers might cancel their phone service, and she notified readers of ongoing efforts by black ministers, organizations, and the *Eagle* to meet with phone company representatives.

In a January 1934 open letter to phone company executives, Bass wrote: "I am asking the Southern California Telephone company if it is possible for a community to grow and expand successfully . . . when one group, even though it is a minority group, of its subscribers are left out of the employment picture on account of race or color."[52] By the following month she was openly advocating phone service cancellations while acknowledging the inconvenience this would cause. "Why not get together and establish a roller skate service," she suggested, possibly tongue-in-cheek: "It certainly would not be as rapid but it would mean that the dollars that we now pour into the telephone company for the upkeep of the same and to pay salaries to young men and women [white of course] in order that they may live decently and respectably according to the American standard, would go to our boys and girls who are often made objects of vice exploiters because the Southern California Telephone Company has closed the door of opportunity in their face."[53] In 1936 after more than a hundred African Americans canceled their telephone service despite the severe inconvenience, the phone company agreed to hire blacks. Several women went to work as telephone operators.

Bass also took on the Wilshire Apartment Service, a white-owned employment agency that hired black women as domestics, worked them for several weeks without pay, and then fired them on flimsy pretenses. She discovered this practice when one victim of the agency came to the *Eagle* offices to complain. After exposing the agency in print, Bass successfully pressed the State Division of Labor Statistics and Law Enforcement to take action against the proprietors. At a hearing on the case, the defendant's lawyer, "a giant of a man, threatened to attack the *Eagle* editor with physical force," Bass wrote.[54]

Although gender was infrequently the focus of Bass's column, she did occasionally feature women's achievements. Fay Jackson was one woman who benefited from Bass's attention and support. Jackson worked at the *Eagle* as an editorial writer in the late 1920s and early 1930s, one of several women who held prominent positions. She, like Bass, penned hard-hitting columns. In one, she wrote: "Here in Los Angeles we are in a peculiar position. The town is populated with southerners who undoubtedly brought their prejudiced program with them. At every session of the legislature attempts are made to inject one form or another of discrimination into the affairs of government."[55] When Jackson quit the *Eagle* and went to work at the Civil Liberties Journal, Bass praised her "superior newspaper ability," saying, she "no doubt will find a place in the Los Angeles newspaper realm for the new baby."[56] Other women who worked for Bass included Vera Jackson, a photojournalist; Ruth Temple, a doctor who provided medical advice; and Idell Bateman, who worked as business manager.

Bass's front-page column provided her with a ready-made platform to discuss issues of importance, but her personal stamp can be seen on the remainder of the paper as well. By the 1930s she was using the *Eagle* as a forum to promote women's capabilities. The paper frequently featured women who earned honors in school, who graduated from college, and who succeeded in nontraditional occupations. The latter included Juanita Edwards, only the second African American policewoman in Los Angeles. In her story Bass noted that Edwards had struggled against heavy odds to get hired. She had to score far higher on civil service tests than whites to get the job, the *Eagle* noted.[57] Another story detailed the career of African American evangelist Maggie J. Whitley, comparing her favorably to famed white evangelist Aimee Semple McPherson. A third detailed the trailblazing exploits of pilot Willa Brown, a "lieutenant and adjutant in the Civil Air Patrol." And a fourth featured Bessye Bearden, "one of the first black women hired by the Internal Revenue Service."[58]

Like white papers, the *Eagle* carried articles that reinforced some "traditional" ideas about women – recipes, fashion notes, stories about parties, and advice columns. For the *Eagle*, however, presenting black women as concerned with recipes, clothing, and children represented an attempt to show that they were not different from, and hence not inferior to, white women. At work Bass did not reflect the feminine image of either black or white womanhood in her dress or mannerisms. She wore loose and nondescript clothing, was stout, pinned her hair back with clips, and frequently was stained with printer's ink. When moving about town at various functions, however, she dressed up and wore heels, nice dresses, and hats.

Articles and columns in the *Eagle* seldom challenged traditional ideas of women as nurturing and maternal, but Bass subtly tweaked these stereotypes. For a few years in the 1930s, the *Eagle* carried an unsigned advice column, "Advice to the Lovelorn," under the pseudonym "Mme. Freezia." The name probably refers to the African-originated flower "freesia." Bass likely wrote the columns herself for they seem to reflect her own sentiments about gender roles. If Bass did not write the columns, she approved their publication. Like similar columns in the white mainstream press, Mme. Freezia offered advice on relations between men and women, but with a decidedly feminist twist. In November 1931 a reader named "Jack" wrote to the columnist:

I have been going out with a girl in whom I am very much interested. A number of times when I have tried to take her out, she has said that she was busy, but I have learned that she went out with somebody else. I don't want her to go out with other men. What shall I do?

Mme. Freezia responded:

Probably you can't do anything about it. I am told that way back in pre-historic ages men were able to prevent women from doing what they wanted to do. Those days have gone. They are going to stay gone.

Another reader asked Mme. Freezia how to stop arguments with her boyfriend, who always took the opposite side of an issue, then refused to stop arguing until she backed down. "If I don't let him think that he has convinced me, he gets angry and stays that way for days." Mme. Freezia responded: "You went wrong when you began to give in to him. Never let a man think that he has convinced you of anything when you know you are right." To a reader requesting advice on whether she should vote for a candidate of her own choosing or for her husband's choice, Mme. Freezia responded that "every person of legal age has a right to vote for whomever they please, and neither your husband nor anyone else has any right to chastise you."[59]

Bass illustrated her strong ideas about women's capabilities in *Eagle* stories that depicted her own exploits. If she ever felt foolish, insecure, or, as a woman, inappropriate for her outspoken and pugnacious attitude, she never spoke of it. In fact, she seemed to revel in her ability to elicit comment and controversy. And she was not shy about heralding her achievements and community honors, which came frequently by the 1930s. In 1934 the African American community in Los Angeles honored Bass on her birthday. The paper did not note which birthday was being celebrated. The story, which bore the initials R. H. M. as a byline, noted that the gathering started out as a "compliment in a small way," but grew into "one of the most outstanding affairs in the entire history of this community. . . . People from all walks of life and all races were there in large numbers to pay their respects to this intrepid pioneer in the uplift and progress of mankind."[60] In 1939 the *Eagle* carried an announcement that an African American sorority, Zeta Phi Beta, was honoring Bass as the "most outstanding woman in Los Angeles with a testimonial banquet." Despite the fact that four names were submitted for consideration, "Mrs. Bass was the unanimous choice of the group."[61]

Bass also publicized speeches she gave and her participation in a variety of local and national groups. In 1938 a front-page story declared a radio address given by Bass to be "No fumbles and all touchdowns." Her "predictions have rung true one hundred percent."[62] The following year, a headline bannered: "EAGLE EDITOR-PUBLISHER DELIVERS SPARKLING ADDRESS IN SAN DIEGO."[63] Bass also created a local weekly radio program in the late 1930s, "The Eagle Newspaper of the Air," offering international, national, and local news from the black press. She proudly promoted the program and her role in it.

From Publisher to Politician

By the early 1940s Charlotta Bass was an institution in black Los Angeles. This can be seen from the financial support the *Eagle* received from African American entertainers such as film stars Dorothy Dandridge and Hattie McDaniel, who held fund-raisers and occasionally helped to subsidize the paper when advertising revenue was low, as it frequently was.[64] Bass may have spoken for the disenfranchised, but her presence was also felt in the city at large as she began to move in larger political circles. Between 1940 and 1945 she represented the Los Angeles Chamber of Commerce at the Chicago Negro Exposition, was appointed western regional director of Wendell Willkie's Republican presidential campaign, became the first African American – man or woman – to serve on a local grand jury, launched a battleship named after African American activist and writer James Weldon Johnson, and ran, unsuccessfully, for city council. She continued to fight for racial justice, lobbying intensively for black employment on city streetcars and in defense plants and struggling to end residential apartheid represented by restrictive covenants.

Through the first half of the decade she stood safely, if

pugnaciously, within the parameters of acceptable activism in the African American community. She was a Republican who occasionally voted for Democrats, including Franklin Roosevelt. But in the latter half of the 1940s Bass began to move outside the bounds of acceptable discourse and abandoned mainstream politics for the leftist Progressive Party that challenged the free market capitalist system and promoted a worldwide order based on interracial cooperation in pursuit of economic justice. By the end of the decade Bass had become controversial, not altogether respectable for cautious black political leaders. She was someone, amid the growing intolerance that characterized the early Cold War period, to be feared as a Communist sympathizer, along with actor Paul Robeson, a longtime friend of Bass's. By this point, however, she cared little about what other people thought, since she had long ago won the battle of convincing men that she could succeed in their world.

The catalyst for Bass's radicalization was World War II. For white women journalists the war represented the last major obstacle to their acceptance as front-page reporters. For Bass, the war brought more personal challenges. First, she had to decide, along with other black publishers, whether to support a conflict in which African American soldiers were asked to fight to preserve a "democracy" that denied them basic rights. She supported the war, but her continuing efforts to connect the fight against Hitler abroad and the fight for civil rights at home led to visits by the FBI and threats to her ability to continue publishing.

Second, she lost her beloved nephew, John Kinloch, a budding journalist and political activist killed in 1945 while fighting the Nazis in Germany. Bass helped to rear her nephew from his early teens and was grooming him to take over as publisher of the *Eagle* after the war. This deeply personal loss may have been the ultimate force that freed Bass from adherence to traditional ideas and behavior.

Although the war served as her crucible, Bass began

connecting larger world events to local race issues long before the United States became involved. In a November 1939 "On the Sidewalk" column, she described a homecoming week celebration at the University of Southern California at which fraternities created an African village and a Jewish merchandizing mart. "Gaudily painted figures of black savages wearing football helmets peer out from apertures of the huts," she wrote. "Another bore the sign, 'Cantor and Cohen food shops, Inc.'"

Bass went on to lament: "Whether the display was the outgrowth of deliberate Nazi sympathies or simply a bent for youthful pranks, it all adds up to the same thing. If the usc boys built their lawn tableau innocent of any serious motives, they betray a very tragic lack of knowledge in the fundamentals of Americanism."[65]

As World War II approached for the United States Bass expressed consternation and anger at the rampant discrimination directed against black workers and prospective soldiers. Along with other African American publishers, she participated in the effort – led by Brotherhood of Sleeping Car Porters head A. Philip Randolph – to convince President Franklin D. Roosevelt to create a Fair Employment Practices Commission by threatening a June 1941 march on Washington. In July 1941, after the creation of the FEPC averted the march, Bass offered an angry appraisal of white attitudes toward black enlistment in the military:

I suppose Negroes should be thankful for small favors. At least that was the impression I got yesterday when a Naval officer visited the plant of this newspaper and handed over a sheet of 'Information for Color-Men regarding Enlistment in the Messmen Branch of the U.S. Navy'....

The sheet was further enlivened with two photographs of Negroes, clad in white cook-jackets, performing [scullery] work. In one shot, a young man was stirring a bowl of some concoction; in the other, a mature, handsome Negro was wiping a knife.[66]

In January 1942 she discussed the hypocrisy of America selling itself to the world as a beacon of democracy. "America has joined England and Russia in 'an attempt to stamp out Nazism throughout the world.' Yet England and the U.S.A. think alike on the subject of race superiority." Russia, on the other hand, "thinks as Roger Williams, son of a London tailor...who was the champion of man's right to worship as he saw fit."[67]

But criticism of the United States did not mean Bass ignored Nazi atrocities, or that she encouraged African Americans to stay out of the conflict. An *Eagle* editorial column by Chandler Owen, publisher of the magazine *Messenger*, noted that: "Negroes used to sing an old sorrow song. 'Before I'd be a slave, I'd be buried in my grave and be carried back home to my mother.' Well, if Hitler wins, get ready to be carried back home to our mother for all the conquered peoples under Hitler are actually being enslaved."[68]

Bass promoted African American involvement in the war effort from the first days of involvement in December 1941, but she continued to link participation to race gains at home. In one 1942 "On the Sidewalk" column she wrote:

The four million Negro people in America at the time of the Civil War showed us how to take advantage of the floodtide of history. Long before the signing of the Emancipation Proclamation, Negroes had seized the initiative in the war against the Confederacy and were ready to do their part when freedom and the Union soldiers came their way.

We must stand in the forefront today in demanding full freedom and full citizenship rights. But we fight with ballots, not bullets, in this war.[69]

In many ways the war enabled Bass to step up her longstanding campaign against organizations such as the Ku Klux Klan and other white separatists. Segregated and inferior housing became her primary focus. Los Angeles, like many other towns and cities across America, imposed restrictive covenants, contracts that barred homeowners in white areas from selling to minority home buyers. Since her earliest days as *Eagle* publisher Bass had fought for homeowners on an individual basis, alleging that such contracts violated the Fourteenth Amendment of the Constitution. "Because the black masses were forced into restricted areas, they became victims of the landlords and of the real estate brokers," Bass wrote. "What would purchase a cozy nook in Hollywood would buy only a tumble-down shack on the Eastside."[70]

During the war she mounted a campaign to outlaw restrictive covenants by forming the Home Owners Protective Association to publicize violence directed at blacks who sought to live in white areas and to lobby local and state government officials. In her column and throughout the *Eagle*, Bass used language and imagery designed to elicit comparisons to Hitler's Germany. "What we are witnessing," Bass wrote in one column, "is a terrible conspiracy engineered by a handful of Fascists." When a judge ordered one black family to vacate their home in a white neighborhood, Bass urged them to stay and fight. For disobeying the order, the family went to jail. Bass then helped to organize a picket line outside the home. The protest grew to more than one thousand, and she called in national civil rights and labor organizations to help. The ensuing national publicity won the family the right to stay in their home, and in 1948 the U.S. Supreme Court ruled restrictive covenants "unenforceable."[71]

Bass joined other civil rights activists in protesting treatment of Mexican American youths targeted by police in the so-called Zoot Suit Riots of 1943 that left dozens of them injured and in jail. Her activism netted her surveillance by the FBI, which kept a close watch on publications deemed a threat to national security during World War II. Agents visited the *Eagle* offices in March 1942 and kept close tabs on Bass's activities throughout the war; the FBI ultimately amassed a 563-page file on Bass. The FBI and postal service

lobbied to revoke mailing privileges of Bass and other assertive African American publishers, but Attorney General
Francis Biddle denied this request.[72] Although Bass was allowed to continue publishing, the experience soured her on
the political system she had long worked to reform from
within.

The disjuncture between America's democratic image
and the ugly realities of racism fueled Bass's growing cyni-
cism, but the death of her nephew John S. Kinloch seems to
have provided the final spark. It brought the contradictions
home in the most personal way possible. Kinloch was the
son of Bass's sister, and he came to Los Angeles from New
York to live with his aunt while he was in his teens. He became her traveling companion, and she was grooming him
as a journalist. He became active in the Los Angeles branch
of the NAACP, helping to form a Youth Council and acting as
its leader. When Bass started her radio program, Kinloch
served as a commentator.

The *Eagle* promoted his activities along with Bass's. When
Kinloch was tapped to speak at graduation ceremonies for
Polytechnic High School in Los Angeles in January 1939, the
headline read: "Editor's Nephew to Speak at Commencement."[73] Kinloch enlisted in the Army in 1943 and was sent
to Europe, where he transmitted dispatches from the front
as a correspondent for the African American press. He was
killed in combat in Germany in 1945. In her autobiography
Bass spoke with pride of Kinloch. "Before he went off to war,
where he gave his life in defense of his country, he set new
and high standards in both policy and program among Los
Angeles youth."[74]

After Kinloch's death Bass began to abandon mainstream
society and politics. She did this slowly, however. In 1945
she ran for Los Angeles City Council as an independent. In
the *Eagle*'s pages she couched this decision in her usual
assertive way, with three stories announcing her candidacy.
She declared that "last Monday night, the people in the Sev-

enth Councilmanic district . . . decided I should seek nomination and election to city council as their representative.
I am not hesitant in accepting the honor."[75] Her platform
called for collective bargaining, low-cost public housing and
health programs, and child care centers and recreational
facilities to prevent juvenile delinquency. She was supported by a broad coalition including labor, black churches,
and business representatives, although the comments of
one backer, a minister, suggest that Bass's personality was
not for everyone. The Rev. Raymond Henderson declared
himself, "Thrilled to second the nomination of Mrs. Bass . . .
whether you like her personally is beside the point."[76] She
lost the election, but in defeat noted that, "I know there is a
new Negro coming of this war and out of prevailing racial
problems."[77]

Two years later Bass renounced mainstream politics and
joined the fledgling Progressive Party, led by former Franklin Roosevelt vice president Henry Wallace. She explained
her change of heart: As an activist in the Republican Party in
the early 1940s, "I discovered two worlds – one upstairs for
white Republicans and down below was the world for Negro
Republicans." While Franklin Roosevelt was alive Bass had
faith in the Democrats, but by the latter 1940s the party had
fallen "into the hands of lesser men. I saw it become the
party of Truman and war, of Rankin and the poll tax. There
was no future for my people in the Democratic party either."[78] In a 1947 *Eagle* column, she wrote: "We cannot follow
old political labels any longer."[79]

The following year she served as national co-chairwoman
of Women for Henry Wallace, when the former vice president ran for president on the Progressive Party ticket. The
new party promoted a platform of civil rights for African
Americans and announced a willingness to go far beyond
remedies proposed by the two mainstream parties. "I am
here to say that Jim Crow in America has simply got to go,"
Wallace announced to his followers.[80]

At this point, the African American *Sentinel,* run by more mainstream publishers and editors, became the dominant newspaper in Los Angeles. Although its editors continued to speak respectfully of Bass, other prominent African Americans in the city were less reluctant to disparage her. For example, Le Roy Ingram, secretary of the Eastside Chamber of Commerce, charged in testimony before the Tenney Committee, California's legislative equivalent to the red-baiting House Un-American Activities Committee, that Bass "interested herself in Communist-front organizations." Before the war, according to Ingram, the *Eagle* had been a respected newspaper. But now it was "a communist propaganda sheet."[81] In spite of such statements, Bass never joined the Communist Party.

In 1951, as she prepared to sell the *Eagle,* Bass reflected on her long experience as a newspaper publisher; she declared both her disillusionment with a political system that aimed to shut down dissent and her optimism about the future: "The American fascists want and need thought control in order to enable them to fasten a police state upon the country. Therefore, they threaten the continued existence of all newspapers, which tell the people the truth. But all through the years, despite such disillusionment I have gotten my greatest inspiration and encouragement from my people, from the working people, who are the true heroes of today."[82]

Bass told her readers that she planned to take it easy, but this was not to be. In 1952 San Francisco attorney Vincent Hallinan tapped her as his running mate for the third party now called the Independent Progressive Party. Between 1948 and 1952 the remnants of the Progressive Party turned much farther to the left than Wallace originally intended and lambasted both mainstream political parties as militaristic and imperialistic. The new Progressives knew they had no chance of winning the election, but with her selection Bass became the first African American woman to run for national office. The mainstream white press had a field day with her. *Time* magazine described her, in derogatory and gendered terms, as "dumpy, domineering," and a power in California Republican ranks until 1940. "Childless," the magazine added, "Mrs. Bass was steered left by a young nephew she adored, [and] became bitterly radical when her nephew was killed in World War II."[83]

This demeaning characterization failed to mention Bass's long career in journalism, a career that gave her a powerful presence in a black community that used the pages of the *Eagle* to fight discrimination, and that made her some white liberal friends as well. Seen in middle-class, white male terms, Bass may have been "dumpy and domineering," but for African Americans and others she represented a woman who faced life on her own terms, who challenged every stereotype, and who happily made powerful enemies as well as friends in the pursuit of causes in which she believed. Throughout her life Bass never backed down from controversy or threat, traits that were not embraced by the male power structure in the late 1940s and early 1950s.

But Bass knew her audience, and most of them weren't readers of *Time* magazine. Instead, they were ordinary people forced to confront a racist system. Bass's lifelong crusade was to prod her audience to challenge this system and to reshape larger cultural ideas about race. But she attempted to reshape their ideas about gender as well through personal example, the issues she featured, the staff she hired, and the ideas she promoted.

Several years after her 1969 death, Bass's friends gathered to dedicate a room to her memory at a Los Angeles library. Robert C. Reed, a minister, wrote a tribute. Calling her a "Mountain of a Woman," he asked, "How many causes did you champion? What battles did you win? The number is legend."[84]

Agness Underwood interviews a female in-
mate inside a California women's prison,
early 1940s. Underwood befriended many
women criminals and portrayed them in
her stories as complex human beings apart
from their criminal activities. This approach enabled her to scoop other journalists on numerous crime stories. Courtesy
of the Agness M. Underwood Collection,
Urban Archives Center, University Library,
California State University, Northridge.

4. Murder Was Her Beat

The Career of Agness Underwood

In the twenty-fifth anniversary edition of the *Los Angeles Evening Herald and Express*, published October 27, 1936, managing editor J. B. T. Campbell set aside one page to allow readers to see the journalists behind the stories: the reporters who covered Los Angeles in all its grit, grime, and glory. He described his staff as though he were taking a page from one of the numerous and colorful films of the 1930s centered on newspaper journalism, "These news hunters live high drama. They are the adventurers of a commonplace world. They stand on the last real frontier of the old Bohemia."

He followed this overview with his own assessment of individual staff members. Of city editor Captain ("Cappy") Marek, Campbell wrote, "He lives front pages and circulates where front pages come from. He burns his candles recklessly to read the beloved word 'Extra' over 'scoops' he has inspired." Star crime reporter "Slim" Connelly was "fat and generally jolly. Most persons in this city have read his 'True Crime Detective Stories' and have shivered as Connelly took them through dark streets to strange lairs." Reporter Gilmore Millen "writes like a bear and writes like a poet. He sorrows as he writes a tragedy. He laughs aloud at his typewriter as he writes a comedy."

Only two of the twenty featured reporters were women – Caroline Walker and Agness Underwood. Walker held a stereotypically female job on the paper. She specialized in society stories, and her columns reflected "the worthwhile things that splendid women are doing in worthwhile organizations," according to Campbell. Underwood, however, was a different story. Her beat was murder, and the more colorful the better. "She should have been a man," noted Campbell. He went on to depict her as "a rip-snorting, go-gettum reporter that goes through fire lines, trails killers, weeps with divorcees and rides anything from airplanes to mules to reach that spot that in newspapers is usually marked with an arrow or an X."[1]

At the time Campbell wrote these words, Underwood was thirty-four and a veteran of ten years in the newspaper business. A short, sturdy woman with a square jaw, a pugnacious appearance, and a ready grin, Underwood probably agreed with this sentiment because she took note of the remark in her 1949 autobiography, *Newspaperwoman*.[2]

What Campbell's words did not and could not have conveyed, however, was how long and difficult the road to acceptance had been for Underwood and the strategy that enabled her to succeed in front-page journalism. In addition to overcoming the longstanding newsroom prejudice against women, Underwood, a wife and mother of two when she became a reporter, also had to overcome the deeply ingrained notion that mothers should stay at home with their children. When asked, Underwood usually understated the obstacles her gender had placed in her way. And she adamantly denied having any feminist agenda or tendencies in pursuing a career in front-page journalism. "I am no feminist," she proclaimed in the first sentence of her autobiography.[3]

Her book was designed to entertain and impress, rather than to delve into difficult and deep issues such as gender. Underwood presented herself in humble terms, as a "barnyard kind of general assignment reporter."[4] But pride in her accomplishments shone through on every page. She depicted herself as having more in common with men than women, but some of her most significant journalistic experiences related to women. Her first and most important mentor, Gertrude Price, was a woman. She counted women among her most celebrated, and her most notorious, subjects. The former included the mother of famed evangelist Aimee Semple McPherson, aviator Amelia Earhart, and fan dancer Sally Rand. The latter included Hazel Glab and Nellie Madison, women who killed their husbands, and Louise Peete, who killed two men before becoming one of the few women executed for her crimes in California.

Underwood reveled in her achievements, but between the lines it is impossible not to see the effort she mounted, from her first days in journalism, to overcome real barriers. This effort centered on making gender a nonissue in the workplace. In many ways Underwood's overall strategy resembled that of her female peers. She exhibited a hyper-vigilance about being perceived as professional at all times and did not risk making public pronouncements about the capabilities of women to strive for nontraditional careers or to combine work and motherhood.

Like many other front-page women Underwood staked out a stereotypically masculine beat on her newspaper and obsessed about gaining the kind of scoops that men boasted about to each other. She distanced herself from the "sob sis-ter" sobriquet. Discussing how she approached the suspect in one particularly grisly murder, she noted: "A sob sister could have wept with and over Manley. . . . To hell with that. I'd rather have a fistful – an armload – of good, solid facts."[5]

But Underwood went even further than most of her fe-male peers to distance herself from female stereotypes, spe-cifically the notion that women were too fragile and demure for front-page reporting. She adopted aggressively "male" language as well as mannerisms and behavior. She drank and swore – "Gahdammit" seems to have been her favorite word – and engaged in slapstick physical humor. She de-scribed one humorous incident in a magazine interview in the 1940s. "A printer had given me a barracuda and I put it in a tank of water in the dark room. . . . I pulled that slimy fish out of the tank and walked up to (the city editor) with it behind my back. 'Lewie, you're a sonofabitch,' I shouted. Then I smacked him across the face with the fish."[6]

Underwood went out of her way to demonstrate that she was tougher than any man when it came to the more gruesome aspects of her stories. "I was no sissy in my control of my reaction to blood and guts," she wrote, going on to describe one story in which police discovered two rotting corpses on a living room sofa. While male reporters and police officers stood around outside, waiting for the house to air out, Underwood went in, climbed over the bodies, and retrieved the victims' identification, then phoned in her story. "Later I sent my brown wool dress to the cleaners," she wrote, "but the odor persisted."[7]

Her style of dress reflected the public image of male front-page reporters – slapdash and shabby – rather than the tailored and neat clothing favored by many celluloid female reporters, including Rosalind Russell's Hildy Johnson in *His Girl Friday*. She wore rumpled and unremarkable dresses, no makeup, and comfortable low-heeled shoes. Colleagues recalled that her hair often looked as if it had been combed with an electric mixer. "She was a raggedy-looking woman," said Jack Smith, a high-profile Los Angeles journalist and columnist, who worked for Underwood for several years.[8]

But Underwood tried to turn her gender to her advantage in some ways as well, by reinforcing traditional ideas about women as compassionate, nurturing, and selfless. She bought her male colleagues thoughtful gifts, sewed on wayward buttons, and listened sympathetically to their personal and professional problems. She labored to turn her newsroom colleagues into an extended family. She invited male reporters and editors home for spaghetti dinners and card games. And she brought her children into the newsroom to distribute presents during holiday seasons.

Underwood's unique approach to her job might have been rooted in survival skills that she learned during a difficult childhood and adolescence. But it might also be attributed to her savvy recognition that her rough edges and scrappy kid-sister persona could actually serve to her advantage in a job that required dogged persistence and the ability to relate to people from all walks of life. Whatever the underpinnings of her approach, from the early days of her career, Underwood saw the big picture. She saw that she needed to craft a strategy that would compel her colleagues to view her as an exceptional journalist who just happened to be a woman, but who "should have been a man."

Her strategy succeeded beyond what she could have dreamed as a young married woman, when she walked into the *Los Angeles Record* in 1926, looking for a job, as she later put it, to pay for a pair of silk stockings. Underwood's autobiography, which she said she wrote at the urging of publisher Harper *&* Row, is a testament to her success, to the acceptance of her peers, and to the notion that a larger audience also saw her as a pioneer with an interesting story to tell. By the time her autobiography was published, Underwood had risen through the paper's ranks to become, at forty-seven, the *Herald and Express*'s city editor, the first woman in the country to hold such a position at a large metropolitan daily. She had become a legend in local newspaper circles and was the recipient of many awards given to women in journalism.

But she never set out to become a career woman, Underwood declared in her autobiography. In fact, "if asked what I regard as the woman's place, I'd probably give the old-fashioned answer: in the home." She would have stayed there herself, Underwood insisted, except that "twenty-two years ago, I got a bear by the tail and couldn't let go. Newspapering has become my life and I fear I'd be miserably unhappy if . . . I should forego, or be crowded out of, my calling."9

Underwood's Path to Journalism
If embracing her *Herald and Express* colleagues as family represented a large part of Agness Underwood's strategy, it may

have been unconscious, and for deeply personal as well as for professional reasons. She was an orphan who spent her childhood years in foster homes and with relatives, all of whom eventually abandoned her. These circumstances made her tough, but they also fueled a need for emotional connections. She found these with her colleagues in the newspaper business, and, strange as it may seem, with law enforcement personnel and some of the criminals whose misdeeds sat at the heart of her stories. Her connection to this latter group gave her access to sources who refused to talk to anyone else, thus reinforcing the idea that she was a truly exceptional reporter.

Many of Underwood's most interesting stories centered on female criminals. She seemed to have had a particular affinity for them, perhaps seeing in them the kind of life she might have had if she had not been lucky enough, and strong enough, to find work that she loved and for which she was suited. Underwood's life story was interesting enough to have filled the pages of any metropolitan daily newspaper, as interesting, in fact, as many of her subjects' lives.

Agness Wilson was born in 1902 in San Francisco and moved to Illinois as a very young child. Her mother died when she was six, and her father sent her and her younger sister to live with relatives in Indiana. After her father died, she lived in a number of foster homes. In one home she recalled being forced to do housework while the parents' three natural children played outside. At fifteen Underwood quit school and went to work, earning six dollars a week. She had to give part of her money to her foster mother. "I felt unloved and alone," Underwood recalled.[10]

Still in her mid-teens she decided to move to San Francisco, where a relative of her father's lived. After a brief stay this relative forced her out. Underwood recalled spending one frigid November night sitting on a park bench in Union Square, clutching her suitcase, eating taffy she purchased with her last dime, and crying uncontrollably. In the morning a kindly woman happened upon her, took pity, and directed her to a Methodist girls' home.[11]

After a few weeks at the home she moved to Los Angeles to live with yet another relative, who had aspirations of turning Underwood into a child actress in the burgeoning film industry. "She put big bows in my hair, dressed me so that I looked younger than my sixteen years, and traipsed me around to the film studios." When her relative realized Underwood was "hopeless as film fodder," she ordered her to get a job, then "wadded my few belongings in newspapers and left the bundle on the front porch."[12] This time she ended up at a Salvation Army facility where she met another struggling teenager, Harry Underwood. Out of fear that she would be turned into authorities for living on her own and being underage, she accepted Underwood's marriage proposal. She was seventeen and he was eighteen.[13] "I was a waitress and he was a soda-jerk," she wrote. "We were determined to establish ourselves in bustling, babbling Los Angeles."[14]

Seven years later in 1926, she was the mother of two – a four-year-old daughter and a one-year-old son – when she decided to apply for temporary work as a fill-in switchboard operator at the *Los Angeles Record*. As she recalled in her autobiography, "I was seeking nothing more than a chance to fortify my family with a few extra dollars. . . . Like many other young married folks in 1926, we were having trouble making ends meet."[15] The *Record*, owned by the Scripps Howard national newspaper chain, was one of six papers in Los Angeles in the 1920s and was one of the smallest. The three largest papers were the *Los Angeles Times* and two papers owned by William Randolph Hearst – the *Examiner* and *Herald and Express*. The *Record* was later absorbed by another paper, the *Daily News*.

Although not initially hired as a reporter, Underwood

quickly became enamored of the newsroom and its male denizens, calling the entire package "raucous, cluttered, profane." Men in short sleeves sat at splintered and scratched desks and pounded on battered typewriters. "I thought I smelled liquor," she wrote.[16] During the last week of Underwood's temporary assignment, Gertrude Price, the *Record's* women's page editor, asked her to help with the newsroom's annual Christmas basket campaign, a relief effort for the poor in Los Angeles. Price became her mentor and gave her more and more work and encouraged her to try her hand at journalism.

Reading Underwood's comments about Price in her autobiography, it is possible to see a covert yet sophisticated gender-based network operating. It was safe for Price to mentor Underwood because she worked in the traditional women's side of journalism. And Price's traditional role made it easy for Underwood to extol her as a mentor. She was much less forthcoming about her relationship with other front-page women journalists throughout her long career, except to note some of them in passing: Marjorie Driscoll of the *Los Angeles Examiner*, Florabel Muir of the *New York Daily News*, and Adela Rogers St. Johns of the Hearst newspaper chain.[17]

Muir was the only female reporter, other than Price, whose work Underwood elaborated on. "She is a hard-hitting, hard-working, square-dealing reporter whose presence on an assignment indicates that top news is breaking," Underwood wrote.[18] Other than Muir, her discussion of women in front-page journalism leaned heavily toward the general, rather than the specific. And the discussion seemed designed more to deflect controversy and discussion rather than to attract it. She declared, for example, that many women "are competent all-around newspapermen – I use the term as inclusive of both genders."[19]

If the few references to women in her autobiography seem aimed at tantalizing the reader with the admission that Underwood saw female "newspapermen" as exactly like and equal to their male colleagues, her next words seem designed to muddy the waters: "There is a fallacy by which newspaperwomen, because they are females, are condemned as a class. A seasoned reporter is cautious about all generalizations, and it is incongruous, therefore, when an otherwise experienced newspaperman lapses into condemnation that a little checking would disclose is not substantial."[20]

The fact that Underwood – whose stories were to the point and easy to decipher – chose to obfuscate the issue of women in front-page journalism in her autobiography suggests the heavy responsibility that she still felt, even after hundreds of women had made their way into newsrooms. In 1949 when she wrote her autobiography, she still counted herself as lucky to have made it in a man's world. But she had not made it as a woman, she insisted, wanting other women to understand this fact. "After I was assigned to the city desk," she wrote, "a barrage of females presented themselves to 'take my place' as the woman reporter on city-side. What they evidently overlooked was the fact that . . . I hadn't held down my job because I was a woman."[21]

Underwood, like many of her female peers, understood the perils of promoting front-page journalism as a job suitable for all women, regardless of their personalities or qualifications. Unqualified women posed a threat to those who deserved a chance. Underwood's recognition of this threat is reflected in the words she used to describe women she deemed unqualified, who used feminine wiles to get ahead or who did not play by the unwritten rules of front-page journalism. She called them "girl-wonders," and the words nearly dripped with disdain. She used such a term to describe one female who used sex during an important trial to get information from a source and again to describe a woman who feared appearing too aggressive in questioning a government official. When Underwood asked a pointed question to one official, a girl wonder retorted, 'You can't ask that, what about protocol?' Underwood replied, "The hell with protocol, I repeated the question . . . the girl-wonder shut up. I suppose there are editors who think gals like that are wonderful."[22]

Occasionally she seemed to come close to calling front-page journalism unsuitable for all but the strongest individuals, women or men. In one speech she called the profession "brutal, mean and unkind. You have to dish it out and you have to take it and it's hard to take it. Too many people are sissies and can't take it."[23] If these words sound discouraging there was a purpose to her message. According to Underwood's son, George, she took her job as a role model and professional gatekeeper seriously. "She knew she was one of the top reporters in Los Angeles. When she was named city editor she recognized it was a major accomplishment for a woman. She spoke of it."[24] This recognition seems evident in her autobiography, where she felt obligated to detour occasionally from telling stories of her exploits in order to discuss gender issues. She obviously understood that this topic was one that her female audience would expect her to cover.

Underwood may have been reluctant to talk about women in the profession in general, but this reluctance did not extend to her mentor Gertrude Price. Underwood regarded her with an esteem bordering on adulation. Price gently but persistently built up Underwood's self-confidence during her early days on the *Record*. From organizing Christmas baskets for Price, Underwood moved on to answering her phones and writing letters. Price taught her to stand up to rude callers and to use correct grammar. One day Underwood described how she "drug" a rug across the floor, only to be corrected. Price "explained that the past tense of drag was dragged," wrote Underwood. Then Price suggested, "learn just one word a day. . . . Use that word several times that day.

Then, some future day, when you need the word, there it will be."[25] When the *Record* broke a big story and Underwood phoned her husband with the news, Price quietly told her: "Never do that . . . what if he told someone who mentioned it to the opposition."[26]

Over time Underwood learned how the newsroom operated, that underneath the apparent chaos and din lay a system, and she longed to be part of it. "At home and at the office, I tried to purge my mind of its reportorial yearnings," she wrote. Finally, in late 1927, she approached Price with trepidation. Price's response heartened her, "Yes, Agness, you can be a reporter – if you really want to. What's more, I think you'll make a good reporter."[27] Price put her to work rewriting stories that had appeared in the paper. Within a few months she assigned Underwood to cover women's club activities. Even at this early date, while in the throes of gratitude, Underwood saw this as a second-class assignment. "To me, a reporter meant city-side reporter," she recalled.[28] But she made the best of her assignment and made contacts among prominent people who would remain sources long after she had become a city-side reporter.

Underwood made no mention of her husband's attitude toward her burgeoning career but did note that "I was away from home ten hours or more daily. Thenceforth, on work days, it was pretty much a matter of raising a family by telephone."[29] Though she purported to believe that most women should stay at home with their children, she believed that working actually improved her relationship with her children. "When we were together, we weren't yelling and scrapping with each other," she told an interviewer.[30] She did hire a housekeeper, however, and had her younger sister nearby to help out in an emergency.[31] By the time Underwood wrote her autobiography she was divorced, although former colleagues recall that she and her husband remained friends.[32]

Her male colleagues seem to have been very understanding of her role as mother and wife. Once when she received an erroneous message that her son had been "run over by an automobile," Price and a male reporter in the *Record* sports department rushed Underwood to the scene, only to discover that the boy had merely fallen off his bike. On another occasion when she and her son and daughter were in an automobile accident, her colleagues raised money to help pay the hospital bills. Underwood sometimes took her children on assignment with her. When the Long Beach earthquake struck in March 1933, she bundled up her son and raced to the scene. "I wasn't about to stay home," George Underwood explained in an interview.[33]

Perhaps her colleagues' lack of complaining about her maternal responsibilities can be attributed to the fact that she was willing to work long hours and that she went out of her way to make them comfortable as well. "I stocked needles and thread in my desk and anchored more than one straying button," she wrote.[34] Her fellow journalists' affection can be seen in the nickname they quickly adopted for her, "Aggie." She was initially stung by this, but Price explained to her that it was meant as a compliment.[35]

Underwood's journalism career began to accelerate when she had been at the *Record* four years. The sports department assigned her to cover wrestling, the city desk asked her to rewrite reporters' stories for later editions, and she eventually got her big break, covering a murder case. On May 20, 1931, two Los Angeles power brokers were found shot to death inside the office of one of the victims. A former deputy district attorney was arrested and charged with the murder. Reporters from all of the papers wrote reams of copy about the crime, but Underwood noticed "a couple of gaps" in the . . . coverage. "No one seemed to have interviewed the suspect's parents." Price encouraged her to pursue this angle and she consulted the phone book for listings. After calling "dozens of wrong numbers, I finally located the parents in Highland Park (suburb of Los Angeles) and got an exclusive interview and photographs from them." It was her first front-page story.[36]

By the end of 1931 it was becoming clear that Underwood was an exceptional reporter, one who was able to use her friendly and sympathetic approach to get subjects to open up to her. One such instance occurred in the summer of 1931 when the *Record* sent Underwood to Hermosa Beach, southwest of Los Angeles, to get an interview with Minnie Kennedy, the estranged mother of famed evangelist Aimee Semple McPherson, whose theatrical Los Angeles–based ministry had a worldwide following. The occasion was the surprise marriage of the fifty-two-year-old Kennedy to G. E. Hudson, whom reporters had nicknamed "what-a-man." This flippant, derogatory attitude had soured Kennedy on the press, and it was Underwood's job to soften her up.

As Underwood recalled, she gained Kennedy's confidence by volunteering to iron her wedding dress and to curl her hair, things that women friends did for each other, to ensure that she would look good for photographs. The strategy worked. Several weeks later a competing newspaper broke the story that Hudson had failed to get a divorce before marrying Kennedy. When the story appeared Kennedy disappeared from sight. Male reporters from across the city raced to find her, but Underwood was the only reporter Kennedy would speak to.[37]

At this early point in her career Underwood's helpful and sympathetic approach had not raised her profile enough to make her success the brunt of male anger. This might be attributed to her unfailingly humble attitude and to her reluctance to openly criticize men whose lackadaisical attitudes toward stories seemed to contribute to her ability to gain scoops. But she occasionally hinted at how she really felt about her less hard-working colleagues. She cited one incident from 1932 in which she and two male colleagues rode together to Long Beach to get the story of a jailed man suspected of murder. The men ignored her on the drive down and then ditched her as soon as they arrived at the police station. While the men stood around the jailhouse joking with other male reporters and continuing to ignore her, Underwood established a rapport with two police officers guarding the prisoner. They agreed to grant her an interview, which she quickly conducted then phoned into the paper before her two colleagues ever realized she was gone. According to Underwood she did not gloat over this triumph but quietly rode back to Los Angeles with her colleagues. They were forced to offer her grudging admiration, she noted.[38]

On another occasion the city editor asked her to take on a job usually handled by a male reporter – opening the city desk mail. She dutifully slit open envelopes, jotted future events in a date book, and wrote up several short items, all in a half-hour. The man who usually did the job took more than five hours, she noted. Another time, she was assigned to cover a burial at sea. She took the advice of a seaman and ate a meal before embarking on the journey. While her male colleagues got seasick, she proudly rode out the rocky ocean trip.[39]

Underwood As a Front-Page Reporter

The lessons that Price taught Underwood – to be unfailingly gracious and humble, yet ferociously competitive in pursuit of good stories – fast-forwarded her career in the early 1930s. Her deferential attitude can be seen from the fact that she always called her managing editor "Mister." He had at least two names for her, she told an interviewer. "When he liked me I was 'Agatha.' When he didn't, I was 'madam.'"[40]

As she gained acceptance from male colleagues, Underwood began to enthusiastically embrace the newsroom atmosphere – swearing like a sailor, playing practical jokes, and drinking alongside her colleagues. She became sort of a surrogate "mother" to them and to some of the sources and subjects of her stories. Reading her autobiography and talking to people who knew her, it is evident that she offered a sympathetic ear to almost anyone with a problem, particularly if they were colleagues or potential sources. Whether these strategies were conscious or unconscious, they seem to have defused problems. Underwood continued to get front-page stories and good assignments at the *Record* until 1935, when she was recruited by the larger and more prestigious *Herald and Express*, with a circulation of more than half a million. The fact she was a wife and mother of two children again seems not to have played any role in the paper's recruitment policies.

The *Herald and Express* had more money to spend on reporters, photographers, and stories. The paper was one of two in Los Angeles owned by William Randolph Hearst, the wealthy muckraker and scandalmonger. (The *Herald and Express* and Hearst's other paper, the *Examiner*, merged in the 1960s to become the *Herald-Examiner*.) Underwood was reluctant at first to go to work for Hearst, she said, because of his reputation for exerting strong control over editorial policy in his newspapers and for ignoring objectivity in favor of color and hyperbole. But she soon came to admire Hearst, to identify completely with the *Herald and Express's* energetic approach to journalism, and to cover the soft underbelly of Los Angeles. "Gahdammit," Underwood quoted one of her editors saying, "the *Herald* has thought up the tag on every important crime story in L.A. during the last 35 years."[41] With Underwood, the paper would get a premier crime reporter.

Underwood did not mention it in her autobiography, but in going to work for Hearst she was working for one of the few publishers willing to hire and promote women. Hearst had started this practice prior to the twentieth century when he hired Winifred Black as a stunt reporter during his early years as publisher of the *San Francisco Examiner*. By the 1930s Hearst had many notable women working on his newspapers: Dorothy Kilgallen in New York; Adela Rogers St. Johns in Los Angeles and Washington DC; and Marjorie Driscoll in Los Angeles. He also hired Eleanor "Cissy" Patterson to edit the *Washington Herald* before selling the paper to her in the 1930s.

Like other Hearst papers the *Herald and Express* specialized in a combination of national and local stories aimed at wringing emotion from readers. It had a limited focus on local politics, leaving this to the *Los Angeles Times*. Because Hearst despised Franklin Roosevelt and the New Deal all of his papers provided negative coverage of the Democratic president and his policies. Hearst's longstanding relationship with actress Marion Davies fueled the paper's Hollywood coverage.

Although Hearst papers specialized in scandal, the *Herald and Express's* crime orientation also reflected the Depression-era desire to make readers forget their troubles by focusing on the travails of others. And it reflected the glamorous but shady aura of Los Angeles as depicted in the period novels of writers such as Raymond Chandler and James M. Cain, who told stories of hard-edged women and men who married for money and bought double-indemnity insurance policies to ensure their financial future. They almost always got caught, and their stories made for fascinating reading.

As was the practice with many papers during this time artists at the *Herald and Express* retouched photographs by penciling in eyebrows and coloring in hair on balding subjects. When subjects smoked cigarettes, artists drew in tendrils of smoke curling upward, presenting either a halo or a sinister effect. Photographers carefully set up their shots and then claimed they were "candid." Headline writers used colorful prose and large type over sensational stories. "Test Hints Miss Todd Taken to 'Death Garage,'" read one 1935 headline about the inquest into the mysterious death of actress Thelma Todd." Three young girls raped and killed by a school crossing guard became the "Inglewood Tots." And a Pasadena bridge where several people leapt to their deaths was dubbed "the suicide bridge."[42]

During her first few years at the *Herald and Express*, Underwood carved out a niche for herself by writing about some of these high-profile murder cases. She made friends with law enforcement personnel so that she could get tips on stories and unusual access to prisoners. In at least one case this access allowed her to help "break" the case. In 1936 the wife of Samuel Whitaker, a church organist, was shot and killed as she and her husband returned home from a movie. Whitaker in turn shot and wounded the suspect as he fled. Police arrested the suspect and took him to a hospital prison ward. Underwood and a photographer talked their way into the ward to set up a photo showing Whitaker's response to the capture. Writing about it later with obvious pride in her powers of observation, she said she grew suspicious when she saw the suspect wink at Whitaker. She urged police to re-question the suspect, and according to Underwood, the suspect broke down and acknowledged that Whitaker had planned his wife's murder to collect on an insurance policy.[43]

In her subsequent story on the coroner's inquest into the murder, Underwood wrote:

"An amazing and almost unbelievable story was told today by James Fagan Culver, a 23-year-old transient … when he narrated in detail how Samuel T. Whitaker assertedly induced him to stage a fake hold-up as a 'thrill' for Whitaker's wife, Mrs. Ethyl E. Whitaker, who was shot to death during the purported robbery attempt."

She went on to write that Whitaker, during the inquest, sat "pale and obviously nervously affected." He also "stared icily at Culver, a youth from the Kentucky mountains." Police found $9,000 in insurance policies in Mrs. Whitaker's name, she added.[44]

Many of the murders Underwood covered were perpetrated by women, and she seemed to have had a particular affinity for these criminals, treating them with unfailing respect in the pages of the *Herald and Express*. Other newspapers covered women and their crimes as well but not with the same effort to present them as complex human beings apart from their criminal activities. Underwood never discussed why she chose to focus on women criminals or to portray them in this light. Perhaps she sought only to get good stories and recognized them as outrageous and infamous enough to capture public attention that would accrue to her as well. Perhaps she unconsciously identified with their "outlaw" lifestyles, or she saw in them challenges she might have faced had she not been fortunate enough to marry a sympathetic man and land a career in front-page journalism. Whatever her reason, Underwood's focus on women and crime gave her a specialty that differentiated her from male crime reporters and brought her further attention and professional plaudits.

The first indication that she had a special interest in this subject came in the spring of 1935 when Underwood talked her editors into assigning her a series of stories about women incarcerated at Tehachapi, then the women's maximum security prison in California. The catalyst was the imminent release of Clara Phillips, convicted a decade earlier in the hammer slaying of a woman she believed was her husband's lover. Underwood's subjects also included Burmah White, a teenager who accompanied her husband on a crime spree, and Nellie Madison, sentenced to death for killing her husband as he lay sleeping late one Saturday night in the hotel room where the couple lived.

Underwood's descriptions of the women verged on admiration, although she stopped short of applauding them for being different. She described Phillips, "the dental assistant" at Tehachapi, as "a model prisoner." She briefly mentioned the murder as well as Phillips's "daring escape" from the Los Angeles County Jail after her conviction with "only 51 cents in her possession, no shoes, and only a lavender slip-on dress." Authorities captured her a short time later in Honduras. Phillips had "aged slightly" during her years in prison, according to Underwood. "Threads of gray may be seen in her dark hair, but she still has that rare smile of hers – on certain occasions."[45]

Underwood took a more critical stance toward Burmah White, whom she called "the blonde bandit moll" and "wife of one of Los Angeles's most notorious slain criminals, Thomas White." She and her husband had gone on a robbery spree that left a schoolteacher permanently blinded. But White had changed during the first sixteen months of her prison sentence, Underwood added. She had just passed her twenty-first birthday when Underwood interviewed her. Though she was "hard and still cynical," she had come to understand that she had to pay dearly for her crimes. "I was an example to the youth of this country when I was sentenced for the wrongs I had done," White told Underwood. To pass the time White said she made curtains, read, and rolled her own cigarettes. Underwood concluded by noting that White had loved "possibly too well," and would pay the price, for the next sixteen years, for "that sort of love."[46]

Underwood's coverage went beyond sympathy and respect in the case of convicted murderer Nellie Madison. Her stories helped to get Madison, just ten days from execution, a reprieve from California governor Frank Merriam, in September 1935. "God knows I have done no wrong, and God will see that justice is done to and for me," Underwood quoted Madison saying during her first interview in March

1935. "That thought is the only thing that keeps me going through all of these days, each of which seems years long."[47]

Madison's troubles began in March 1934 when police discovered the body of her husband lying on the floor of the Burbank hotel where the couple lived. She fled and was discovered crouched in a closet in the home of a friend. During her trial, Madison insisted that the person found dead in her hotel room was not her husband, but the jury found this story preposterous and sentenced her to death. Using sympathy and the notion that she could get Madison's case renewed attention, Underwood encouraged Madison to open up to her.

The story she told Underwood seemed almost as preposterous as the one the jury rejected. It turned out that Madison had not been legally married. Her husband had arranged a sham marriage to gain access to money Madison had inherited. She was unaware of this, however, until she unexpectedly returned home one afternoon and discovered her husband in bed with a teenaged girl. After that her husband began beating her; he told her their marriage was a fake and threatened to publicly expose her as a fornicator. The prospect of public shame, along with her husband's raging violence that continued, unabated, for a week following her discovery, led Madison to kill him, she told Underwood. Underwood kept the story, along with efforts to win Madison a commutation, in front of the public for weeks. Days before her scheduled execution, Governor Frank Merriam commuted her death sentence, although she served seven more years in prison. Discussing the case in her autobiography, Underwood again offered evidence of how well she understood gender ideology. Jurors might have sentenced Madison to death, according to Underwood, because she "had been married three times and . . . was childless."[48]

Underwood also became personally involved in the case of Hazel Glab, a female murderer with whom she developed a lasting friendship. When Underwood met Glab in 1936 Glab had just filed a will in the Los Angeles county courts that named her as beneficiary to the estate of her wealthy, elderly fiancé, who had died during a trip to Las Vegas. The fiancé's family challenged the will, and this brought Glab to the attention of police. Glab was not unknown to law enforcement; she had been a suspect seven years earlier in the murder of her husband. All of Los Angeles's daily papers competed for Glab's exclusive story, but Underwood won the contest after tracking down Glab at a local hotel. To thwart other reporters, Underwood took Glab to her own home, where her daughter was hosting a potluck dinner for forty Girl Scouts. Glab happily helped Underwood serve the food and wash dishes, Underwood recalled in her autobiography. Glab was eventually prosecuted and convicted of murdering her husband and forging her fiancé's will, which she had written in purple ink.[49]

Underwood's coverage of the case, while straightforward, was also respectful and sympathetic. "Hazel Belford Glab appeared today in Judge Schmidt's court and with her chin up and, in a loud, firm voice, said: 'I am not guilty'" to charges that she forged her fiancé's will.[50] At the murder trial, Underwood offered flattering portrayals of Glab's demeanor and her courtroom attire. "Dressed in a green suit with brown velvet, her jacket trimmed with brown beaver, the accused woman made a neat and stylish appearance. Her eyes were clear and alert as she leaned forward now and then to whisper to her attorney."[51] She referred to Glab several times as "a former beauty queen," and noted her age as thirty-five, although photographs make it obvious that she was much older.

Underwood downplayed or did not mention some pieces of evidence against Glab in the murder case. She did not mention, for example, that a month before the killing a witness claimed to have heard Glab say she wanted to "bump off her husband." The *Los Angeles Times* did include this information and did not find her to be as sympathetic or attractive a subject as Underwood did. The *Times* reporter characterized her as a "blonde woman, once described as a beauty contest winner and a dancer." The *Times* also described Glab "angrily" watching "the prosecution weave a web of evidence against her."[52]

Jurors did not find her sympathetic either and convicted her of second-degree murder. In April 1936 Glab was taken to the Tehachapi Women's Prison to serve a seven-year-to-life sentence. The *Herald and Express* story depicted a defiant Glab, declaring to those assembled, "Don't say I cried or carried on, because I'll be back." The accompanying photo showed her in sunglasses and carrying a copy of *Detective* magazine.[53]

From Front-Page Reporter to City Editor

By the 1940s Agness Underwood was considered by many in the field to be the "top newspaperman" in Los Angeles.[54] She continued to cover crime stories, including those about women, but also broadened her coverage to include coverage of Hollywood celebrities, some of whom treated her as one of their own. For example, Lee Tracy, who played a front-page reporter in several newspaper genre films, liked to sit in on high-profile murder cases to gain atmosphere for his own characterizations. Underwood seems to have been one of his role models, at least according to her, and he often told friends and acquaintances that he and Underwood had "covered" the trials together.[55] Actress Mary Astor befriended Underwood during an ugly child custody battle between Astor and her ex-husband and gave her exclusive information about her ex-husband's love life.[56] And fan dancer Sally Rand invited Underwood into her bedroom to interview her as she prepared for marriage to rodeo cowboy Thurkel Greenough.[57]

By the 1940s Underwood was on a first-name basis with virtually every political officeholder in the greater Los Angeles region. When she complained that newsreel cameramen were getting better treatment than newspaper photographers in covering breaking news, a Los Angeles official asked, "What can I do for you Agness?" And, during the 1944 paternity trial of Charlie Chaplin, accused of fathering a baby girl out of wedlock, she knew the judge hearing the case well enough to take it upon herself to enter his chambers with a photographer to take a photo of the toddler. Underwood undertook this action because she knew her readers would like to see a photo of the aging actor with the toddler. However, "it took no great perception to realize that Chaplin would probably refuse to pose for a picture with the little girl whose paternity he was denying."[58]

During a court recess, she strode into the judge's chambers where the child was waiting with her grandmother, scooped her up, and carried her downstairs to the courtroom. "I set her on the counsel table between [the defense lawyer] and Chaplin, who looked at the child and then turned away slightly. In that split second, the photos [were] shot. It became a news picture carried by the syndicates to publications throughout the country." A jury subsequently ruled Chaplin to be the child's father, and the court ordered him to pay child support.[59]

By the 1940s the management of the *Herald and Express* realized the public relations value of an Underwood byline. In a notorious 1944 murder case her interviews became a part of the story. The paper carried a photo of Underwood interviewing the murder suspect alongside her questions and the suspect's answers. This particular case fit squarely into the bizarre-but-true crime genre that Underwood so relished, and at which she excelled.

The Louise Peete case was tailor-made for Underwood. When police arrested Peete she was on parole for an earlier murder. During much of her incarceration an elderly Santa Monica couple had cared for her daughter, and Peete moved in with them upon her release in early 1944. After several months the couple began to suspect that Peete was stealing from them and phoned her parole officer. As the wife stood with the phone in her hand, Peete shot and killed her. She quickly checked the dazed husband into a mental hospital, moved back into the couple's home, and began to sell off their property. Her actions eventually aroused suspicions and police arrested her in December 1944.[60]

The *Herald and Express* wasted no time in assigning Underwood to cover the case. Her editors also sent along a photographer – who included a photo of Underwood interviewing Peete alongside her exclusive front-page story. "Mrs. Louise Peete . . . is shown as she gave an exclusive interview to *Evening Herald and Express* reporter Agness Underwood today," read the photo caption.[61] In the interview Underwood made it clear she recognized that she was performing an important task – serving as a sounding board for Peete who proclaimed her anguish at being arrested.

When Peete went on trial Underwood provided generally even-handed coverage, acknowledging that it was "filled with drama and horror." But she portrayed the defendant as stoic and dignified in the face of near-certain conviction. And as a female reporter, she was respectful of Peete's personal vanity. For example, she fought with her editors, who kept trying to insert the fact that Peete was overweight into Underwood's stories. On a personal level she spent a day off of work trying to find a specific shade of eyebrow pencil for Peete to use to cover her graying hair. And she never contradicted Peete's assertion that she was fifty-eight, although she was really sixty-three.[62] Other papers, including the *Los Angeles Times*, did make unflattering references to Peete's appearance and publicly noted her efforts to convince the public she was younger than her real age.[63]

Underwood explained the motives behind her approach, "Why antagonize her thus and ruin a chance-in-a-million?" Underwood declared. "I laid off trying to pin her down about her age – a fine lady is entitled to count her years in the seclusion of her boudoir."[64] This respectful stance once again earned Underwood close access to the defendant. When Peete was sentenced to death she immediately turned to look at Underwood in the courtroom. As Underwood later related the story, Peete "pinched me under the chin and, tearless herself, said, 'now, don't you cry.'"[65] The *Times* reporter also noted Underwood's presence in the courtroom at this critical moment. "Apparently detecting what she thought was a tear in the eye of a woman reporter," the *Times* writer explained, "the defendant stopped on her way out of the courtroom and said, 'don't weep for me, dear.'"[66]

The most significant piece of evidence attesting to Underwood's stellar journalistic status was her promotion to the job of *Herald and Express* city editor. Despite her stature the promotion was unexpected and a shock to Underwood, she said, mostly because the city editor was viewed as the hub around which the entire newsroom revolved. No woman before Underwood had ever held this job at such a large paper.

The promotion came in January 1947, in the midst of one of Los Angeles's most sensational murder cases, dubbed the "Black Dahlia" for the slinky black clothing worn by Elizabeth Short, the young victim. Underwood was one of the first to arrive on the scene after Short's body was discovered in a field. As she described it, the body was neatly sliced in half, "through the abdomen, under the ribs. The two sections were ten or twelve inches apart. The arms, bent at right angles at the elbows, were raised above the shoulder. The legs were spread apart."[67]

Underwood's supreme confidence in herself as a journalist by this time emerges in a story she told in her autobiography about the Black Dahlia case. When police arrested a suspect early in the investigation, the arresting officer suggested the suspect talk to Underwood. She reported the conversation between the two men, "I've known this lady for a long time, on lots of big cases and I can tell you she won't do you wrong." Following her interview Underwood declared her belief that the suspect was innocent, and police let him go. No one has ever been charged in the case.[68]

Underwood may have had a high profile in Los Angeles journalistic circles, but her promotion to city editor earned her attention from major national news magazines as well. *Time* magazine asked her about her first days on the job: "I'd sit there for ten minutes with a handful of clips before I'd have the nerve to ask somebody to go to work on them." In the same article Underwood expressed pride in her reporters, whom she called her "boys," and said she wanted "to sit on the desk and have them call me Grandmaw." The *Time* reporter went on to describe her as a "gregarious soul who 'loves everybody.'" The reporter quoted one of her "boys," who declared that, "Aggie's not a woman, she's a newspaperman. No one would dare send flowers on this occasion. She'd throw 'em at whoever did.[69]

Newsweek also went out to Los Angeles to do a story. The magazine quoted *Herald and Express* managing editor Campbell's characterization of Underwood as "the best newspaperman in town." The magazine briefly summarized her early years, her beginnings in the newspaper business, her many scoops, and her close relationships with Los Angeles officials. "When a jury came in with the verdict on Albert Dyer, rapist-killer of three small girls back in the '30s," noted *Newsweek*, "the judge held up the verdict until the bailiff could summon Aggie from her breakfast in a restaurant across the street from the courthouse."[70] Her reporters "idolize her," the *Newsweek* reporter added, "and she likes to bend an elbow with them after hours at a nearby tavern." The magazine also paid tribute to her path breaking status by noting that William Randolph Hearst himself had sent his granddaughter to Los Angeles to learn reporting from Underwood.[71]

Underwood might have been nervous about making the career leap from colleague to boss, but she never suggested that this feeling had anything to do with gender, or that a man in the same position might not have experienced the same emotions. By 1947 Underwood had enough confidence in her own individual talent that she believed gender had played little or no role in her professional accomplishments. But as in other instances in her autobiography, she understood that readers probably cared about this issue.

The entire discussion of her promotion attests to her apparent concern as to how a public less familiar with her than her colleagues might view her career trajectory. Her protestation about feminism and positive comments about women's traditional roles can be seen in this light. Otherwise why would she deem it necessary to proclaim herself not a feminist on the first line of her book? Or to extol the traditional role of housewife, while declaring that she was unsuited to this role? Or to lament perceived female traits such as "stridency." Women who exhibited this trait "are the kind I'd like to slug with that baseball bat on my desk," she announced.[72]

At the same time taking a page from front-page journalist Dorothy Thompson, Underwood also seemed to wink at the foolishness of these stereotypes by suggesting to her readers the absurdity of believing that a woman could not handle a job as taxing as city editor. For example, in describing her first day on the job Underwood discussed how "employees from other departments crowded into the city room . . . perhaps to check on whether the female city editor would blow her top. I'm afraid they were disappointed. On that and the following day the press run was one million, the greatest in the history of the *Herald*."[73]

If Underwood experienced any reservations or negative comments from male staff members, she never discussed it publicly. Instead she offered glowing reports about her "boys" and testified to her ability to direct the city desk like "an orchestra – and I don't use that baseball bat for a baton."[74] She attributed her success as city editor to her longstanding relationships with *Herald and Express* employees from all levels. "I find that courtesy and respect paid to others, small and great through the years, results today in dividends," she wrote.[75] As evidence of this attitude, she kept a bottle of bourbon in her desk to help reporters get over their hangovers, and she treated reporters to beers when they did a particularly good job. But she also did not take "any back talk, insulting oafing, or smart-aleck insubordination." Jack Smith, who worked for Underwood, recalled years later that "everybody knew she was really something. It was fun to come to work. We would have done almost anything for her."[76]

Throughout the remainder of her long career Underwood's two-sided strategy that combined dogged tenacity and nurturing compassion continued to serve her well. Members of Los Angeles's officialdom offered her respect and admiration. A 1948 article in *The American Policeman*, a Los Angeles–based publication, warned young officers new to the job that Underwood would not be happy to have reporters from other papers gain scoops on stories. So the writer warned them "if a big murder case breaks on your shift and you do not see one of Aggie's reporters around, you had better find one."[77]

She received further promotions and ended her career in 1968 as managing editor of the paper now called the *Los Angeles Herald-Examiner*. But by the 1950s she had begun to soften her individualistic stance and to mentor other women. One of them was editorial assistant Eddy Jo Bernal, who Underwood encouraged to pursue a career in front-page reporting. She also kept letters of correspondence from women who wrote her asking career advice, and she wrote letters of praise to women front-page reporters at other papers. As dozens of photographs she kept in a file attest, she reveled in honors bestowed on her by women's press organizations. One came from the National Federation of Press Women, honoring her as the outstanding woman in journalism for 1962. Even her chief competition, the *Los Angeles Times*, honored her as one of its "women of the year" in 1960.

While Underwood rarely openly acknowledged her part in breaking new ground, others did note her achievement. In 1958 when a Los Angeles osteopathic college asked Underwood to give its commencement speech, she asked celebrity columnist and good friend Walter Winchell to introduce her. His words suggest how well her professional strategy had served her and the larger community of women: "Agness Underwood ... by her own great talents, has won recognition not only for her paper, but for her sex. Few women have ever been trusted so completely and so often with such tremendous responsibility. . . . Her success has validated one of the mighty movements of the twentieth century: the belated acknowledgment that, in the distribution of talent, the Creator endowed women as well as men."[78]

Underwood decided to retire in 1968 when union news reporters went on strike at the *Herald-Examiner*. Although she was a member of the management staff, she did not want to cross a picket line manned by her "boys." Entertainer Bob Hope emceed the testimonial dinner held in her honor that drew a crowd of several thousand. Hope also paid humorous tribute to Underwood's career and her trailblazing status. But perhaps the strongest evidence of Underwood's willingness to link her career success to the larger "group called women"[79] came in 1976, during an interview she gave to a young woman studying for a master's degree in journalism. Interviewer Natalie Holtzman suggested Underwood really had been a feminist after all. Underwood did not contradict her.[80]

Afterword

The hundreds of women who worked as front-page reporters in the 1920s, 1930s, and 1940s did not publicly claim role-model or path breaker status for themselves, nor could they have seen that the years spent working between the lines to chip away at longstanding prejudices and stereotypes would pay large dividends for future generations of women. But their work was indispensable in changing the climate for women seeking journalism careers in the post–World War II period.

Examples of their achievements can be seen in the increasing numbers of women who sought and attained journalism careers, in their achievements, and in the professional strategies of women who entered front-page journalism in the years following World War II. Before the war, only one woman, Anne O'Hare McCormick, had won a Pulitzer Prize. By 1960 four more women had won journalism's top honor: Marguerite Higgins in 1951, Caro Brown in 1955, Mary Lou Werner in 1959, and Miriam Ottenburg in 1960. And by the 1960 census, women made up nearly half of the sixty-thousand-member journalistic workforce.[1]

One of them was Sarah McClendon, who became a reporter in Texas during World War II. In the late 1940s she started her own Washington DC, news service. In her autobiography, McClendon proudly described herself as "pushy" and provided this evidence: at one Dwight D. Eisenhower press appearance in the early 1950s, McClendon leaned over the balcony of the National Press Club and demanded to know whether he would take reporters' questions. In response, reporter Eric Sevaraid declared disdainfully that she "gave rudeness a new dimension." McClendon championed this observation, "My main fault seems to be that I dare to ask what other reporters are only thinking."[2]

The fact that McClendon was in the press club balcony at all represented a leap forward for women by the 1950s. And their place there reflected both how far they had come since the 1930s and how far they still had to go to gain parity with men. By the 1950s they were willing, as a group, to confront the journalism fraternity head on, rather than letting their work do the talking for them.

By this date, although many barriers had fallen for women, they still could not gain membership in the all-male National Press Club. As former *New York Times* reporter Nan Robertson explained in her book *Girls in the Balcony, Women, Men, and the "New York Times,"* all important political figures who gave speeches in Washington made appearances at the press club. Because they were not members, women journalists could not attend these functions and thus were at a disadvantage in trying to report stories on influential people. They began to lobby vociferously for admission, starting in the late 1940s when Helen Thomas of United Press International became president of the Women's National Press Club. "I have been a women's libber all my life," Thomas wrote in her 1975 autobiography. "Once doors opened, I have made it a policy to walk right in."[3]

In 1955 the men caved in, slightly, ruling that women could attend journalistic functions at the press club but only if they remained in the balcony, away from the main events. Robertson called the press club balcony "one of the ugliest symbols of discrimination against women to be found in the world of journalism." It was a metaphor, she added, "for what working women everywhere faced."[4] It took until 1971 for women to be admitted as members of the Press Club.

If they could articulate grievances and lobby for change

better than their predecessors could, front-page women who came to prominence after World War II also understood that the earlier generation had opened the doors for them. Robertson, for example, cited Anne O'Hare McCormick as her inspiration. Robertson became a reporter in 1948 after graduating from Northwestern University. She had longed for a journalism career since high school, when she read stories by McCormick. "Nothing ever gave me a more vivid sense of the 'great striding events' that the likes of Anne McCormick covered than those magnificent wartime front pages," she said.[5] Robertson went on to win her own Pulitzer Prize in 1983 for a series on toxic shock syndrome. Helen Thomas said she also saw the possibilities in a front-page career because of the work done by women like Ruth Finney. "I saw [Finney] at work when I first got to Washington," she explained in an interview. "She and others like her gave me the sense that I could do this too."[6]

The exploits and public presence of front-page women even influenced those who ultimately did not seek careers in journalism. In her 1963 book *The Feminine Mystique*, author Betty Friedan used dozens of personal anecdotes to describe "the problem with no name" that infected so many white, middle-class women homemakers in the postwar period. She quoted one letter from a college student detailing her mother's angst, "she wanted to be a newspaper reporter from the time she was twelve. I've seen her frustration for twenty years."[7]

It was not only white women who benefited from the examples set by their predecessors. African American women reporters also made great professional strides by the 1950s, as a result of the women who went ahead of them. The new generation of African American journalists included Alice Dunnigan and Ethel Payne, both of whom crossed racial as well as gender barriers. Dunnigan was a teacher and writer before she moved to Washington DC during World War II.

In 1946 the *Chicago Defender* recruited her as its Washington correspondent, and by the late 1940s, she had become the first black woman accredited to cover Congress and the White House. In 1951 she was named best "black reporter" in Washington. Like most other black journalists, Dunnigan focused on racial issues in her political coverage, often to the embarrassment of white political leaders. Eisenhower, for example, refused to call on Dunnigan during press conferences for fear she would pointedly question him about race.[8]

Ethel Payne, who wrote for the *Chicago Defender* beginning in the early 1950s, was pushier than Dunnigan in pursuit of civil rights stories. When she arrived in Washington in 1953, she "quickly became known as an aggressive person," she recalled in an interview years later. At one press conference she made Eisenhower almost apoplectic when she asked when he planned to end segregation in interstate travel. A white, male *Washington Post* colleague commiserated with Payne, telling her that he, himself, had earned the president's ire for asking touchy questions.[9]

As Payne's anecdote suggests, by the 1950s white and black journalists had begun to enjoy a more collegial relationship, although the focus of their various journalistic enterprises still differed significantly. During this decade Dunnigan became the first African American admitted to the Women's National Press Club, and Ethel Payne, although she declared herself to be, generally, a "loner" in Washington journalistic circles, made friends with a few white women colleagues, including Sarah McClendon. McClendon did try to go out of her way to be friendly to her, Payne told an interviewer. She "saw me as a woman out there struggling for it."[10]

As their careers and lives wound down, the experiences of Ruth Finney, Charlotta Bass, and Agness Underwood exemplified the changes that they had helped to foster. Finney continued covering politics from Washington DC until 1965. In 1971 a Scripps Howard executive wrote of her career, "Never, never, in all [her career] did Ruth ever write a sob sister story. We never asked her to do the women's angle." Finney wrote her autobiography in the early 1970s, because, she said, she wanted future generations to understand the experiences of earlier generations of women journalists. She was eighty-one when she died in Washington DC in 1979.

Bass died in a Los Angeles nursing home in 1969 at the age of ninety-four. After winning less than 1 percent of the vote as the vice presidential candidate on the Independent-Progressive Party ticket in 1952, she moved to Lake Elsinore in the California desert. She lived quietly but continued to work with women's organizations on behalf of both gender and race issues. She worked with Jewish women's groups to create a library for social change that included books on race relations and on women's rights.

After Underwood retired from journalism in 1968 she continued garnering honors, including the first honorary lifetime membership by the California Newspaper Publishers Association. In its proclamation the CNPA noted that Underwood "has amassed more tributes than any other woman in journalism." By the 1970s she was considered a legend in Los Angeles newspaper circles. Male journalists who had worked for and with her regaled younger counterparts with "Aggie" stories. Among the most rapt members of their audience: young women journalists whose careers she inspired but who could never hope to attain the kind of status she enjoyed in her adopted hometown. Underwood died in 1984 at the age of eighty-two.[11]

In their careers, Finney, Bass, Underwood, and dozens of other female front-page journalists tolerated discrimination, demeaning comments, and inequities while laboring diligently to make themselves acceptable to men who jealously guarded the door into the newsroom. Their strategies when dealing with men were rarely confrontational, often calculating, and ultimately, subversive. By presenting themselves publicly as talented, competent, and independent, yet modest to a fault and willing to play by male rules, they opened the door to subsequent generations of women who no longer demonstrated any inclination to present themselves as anything but talented, competent, and absolutely equal to men.

Notes

Introduction

1. Hill, *Women in Gainful Occupations*, 42; Bureau of the Census, *Sixteenth Census of the United States, 1940*, 3:75; Bureau of the Census, *U.S. Census of Population*, 1950, 2:1–261.

2. Information on the overall percentage of married women in the workforce is from Weiner, *Working Girl to Working Mother*, 101–4. Data on the percentage of married journalists is from Bureau of the Census, *Fifteenth Census of the United States*, 1930, 298.

3. Woloch, *Women and the American Experience*, 382.

4. Rosenberg, *Beyond Separate Spheres*.

5. Rosenberg, *Beyond Separate Spheres*, xiii.

6. Scott, *Gender and the Politics of History*, 60.

7. The mass audience and how it "saw" women is discussed in Lipsitz, *Time Passages*, 169–72. Lipsitz focuses on film, arguing that filmmakers enter a cultural "dialogue" already in process at the time of their creative endeavor, and that their films help to reposition audiences' attitudes about larger cultural and social values. This occurs because ideas are always in flux.

8. A number of African American historians have focused on black women's roles as community leaders and how this impacts gender identity and aspirations as well. They include hooks, *Feminist Theory* and *Ain't I a Woman*; Collins, *Black Feminist Thought*; Giddings, *When and Where I Enter*; and Jones, *Labor of Love*.

9. Bennion, *Equal to the Occasion*.

10. Feminism remains a slippery term. Cott defines it as having three components: A belief in equality, an understanding that gender is socially constructed, and an understanding that women are part of a larger group in which "one's experience reflects and affects the whole." Cott, *Grounding of Modern Feminism*, 4–5. Kessler-Harris discusses the divisions between "equal rights" and

"social" feminists in the years following suffrage in *In Pursuit of Equity*; Ware focuses on the so-called liberal brand of feminism, using flyer Amelia Earhart as an example in *Still Missing*. Grant details the development of "modern" feminist theory in the 1960s and 1970s, arguing that the theoretical underpinnings themselves have created problems and divisions. To create a cohesive movement feminists crafted a language that emphasized women's unique qualities and commonalities. But this was difficult to reconcile with the movement's focus on equality. Grant, *Fundamental Feminism*. Echols also depicts the divisions and conflicts among "second-wave" feminists in *Daring to be Bad*.

CHAPTER ONE: *Crossing the Threshold*

1. Finney, *Careers for Women*, 427–30.

2. Fleischman, *Careers for Women*, 266.

3. Walker, *City Editor*, 249.

4. Walker, "A City Editor's Testament," 25–34.

5. Walker, "A City Editor's Testament," 25–34.

6. Hill, *Women in Gainful Occupations*, 42.

7. Bureau of the Census, *Fifteenth Census of the United States*, 1930, 5:83; Bureau of the Census, *Sixteenth Census of the United States*, 1940, vol. 3; Bureau of the Census, *Seventeenth Census of the United States*, 1950, vol. 2.

8. Logie, *Careers for Women in Journalism*, 41–45.

9. Ross, *Ladies of the Press*, 4–13.

10. U.S. Congress, *Official Congressional Directory*, May 1924–June 1947.

11. *Newsweek*, March 3, 1945, p. 64.

12. Beasley, *Negro Trailblazers*.

13. Smith, *Notable Black Women*. The book lists more than a half-dozen African American women who worked as reporters during this time.

14. Tarry, *The Third Door*, 110.

15. Marvel Cooke, interview by Kathleen Currie, 1989, pp. 68–75, Women in Journalism Oral History Project of the Washington Press Club Foundation.

16. Bass, *Forty Years*, 31.

17. Hill, *Women in Gainful Occupations*, 33–34.

18. McBride, *A Long Way from Missouri*, 160.

19. Scholars who have written general histories about women and journalism include Ross, *Ladies of the Press*; Marzolf, *Up from the Footnote*; Shilpp and Murphy, *Great Women of the Press*; Robertson, *Girls in the Balcony*; and Mills, *A Place in the News: From the Women's Pages to the Front Page*.

20. The number of newspapers is from Emery, Emery, and Roberts, *The Press and America*, 162. Other books that document the rise of big-city journalism include Barth, *City People*; Schudson, *Discovering the News*; Kluger, *The Paper*; and Talese, *The Kingdom and the Power*.

21. Smith and Bogart, *The Wars of Peggy Hull*.

22. Kelly, *Flowing Stream*, 458–59.

23. Leuck, *Fields of Work for Women*, 214.

24. Underwood, *Newspaperwoman*, 3.

25. Duster, *Crusade for Justice*.

26. Duster, *Crusade for Justice*, 33.

27. Marchand, *Advertising the American Dream*.

28. Kessler-Harris, *In Pursuit of Equity*, 40.

29. Ware, *Still Missing*.

30. Kelly, *Flowing Stream*, 460.

31. Emery, Emery, and Roberts, *The Press and America*, 289.

32. Emery, Emery, and Roberts, *The Press and America*, 292.

33. Schudson, *Discovering the News*, 134–48.

34. Emery, Emery, and Roberts, *The Press and America*, 334.

35. Heald, *Transatlantic Vistas*.

36. Davis, *Contributions of Black Women*, 238.

37. Jackson, "The Popular Media," traces the history of African American journalism. Information on Delilah Beasley is included in Smith, *Notable Black American Women*, and in Beasley, *Negro Trailblazers*. And information on African American women journalists is included in Davis, *Contributions of Black Women*.

38. Manning, *Ladies Now and Then*, 119.

39. Dorr, *A Woman of Fifty*, 83.

40. Lowell, *Gal Reporter*, 50.

41. Lowell, *Gal Reporter*, 3.

42. Brody, "Newspaper Girls," 273–76.

43. Ruth Cowan, interview by Margot Knight, 1987, p. 20, Women in Journalism Oral History Project of the Washington Press Club Foundation.

44. Thompson, "Women Correspondents and Other New Ideas," 11–12.

45. Helen Kirkpatrick, interview by Anne S. Kasper, 1990, p. 21, Women in Journalism Oral History Project of the Washington Press Club Foundation.

46. Furman, *Washington By-Line*, 40.

47. *The Nation*, December 1926–March 1927. The articles asked women to discuss their backgrounds and their political beliefs, to determine what factors made women into either feminists or non-feminists. After the series ran, the magazine asked two psychologists – a man and a woman – to offer their own views of feminism. Their essays ran on July 6, 1927. The woman psychologist surmised that oppression and discrimination had driven women to feminism. The male psychologist surmised that the women were disturbed.

48. Underwood, *Newspaperwoman*, 3.

49. Mary Neiswender, interview by author, Long Beach CA, July 9, 2000.

50. Oglesby, "Women in Journalism," 29.

51. Bureau of the Census, *Fifteenth Census of the United States, 1930: General Report on Occupations*, 5:84.

52. Bureau of the Census, *Fifteenth Census of the United States, 1930: General Report on Occupations*, 5:83, 154.

53. Among the best and most recent books on the Roosevelts are Goodwin, *No Ordinary Time*; and the (so-far) two-volume biography on Eleanor Roosevelt by Cook, *Eleanor Roosevelt*. Eleanor Roosevelt's relationship with women reporters is documented in several recent books, most notably Beasley, *Eleanor Roosevelt and the Media*; and Faber, *E. R.'s Friend*.

54. Furman, *Washington Byline*, 277.

55. Finney, "Journey from the Star," 367–69, box 1: folder 5, Ruth Finney Papers (From here on out, the number preceding the colon is the box number, and the number following the colon is the folder number).

56. Faber, *E. R.'s Friend*; Rollyson, *Nothing Ever Happens to the Brave*.

57. Bourke-White, *Portrait of Myself*.

58. Lowell, *Gal Reporter*, 50.

59. Marvel Cooke, interview by Kathleen Currie, 1989, p. 80, Women in Journalism Oral History Project of the Washington Press Club Foundation.

60. Galerstein, *Working Women on the Screen*, 450. Out of 2,000 films examined by Galerstein, not surprisingly, 1,600 featured women in traditional careers. But journalism represented the largest percentage – 130 out of 400 films – in which women worked in nontraditional roles.

61. Sanders, *Dorothy Thompson*, 290–300. Sanders says that Thompson was angry at the film's portrayal of a globe-trotting journalist who could not handle her personal life. But this is how Sanders portrays Thompson. She shows Thompson utilizing the same approach as other, less famous, front-page reporters: proclaiming adherence to domestic ideals, but working to subvert them.

62. Gilman, *Sob Sister*.

63. Iona Robertson Logie, interview by author, Carmel CA, August 1994. Logie's dissertation was published as *Careers for Women in Journalism*.

64. Logie, *Careers for Women in Journalism*, 35–78.

65. Logie, *Careers for Women in Journalism*, 152.

66. Logie, *Careers for Women in Journalism*, 163.

67. Ross, *Ladies of the Press*, 8.

68. Ross, *Ladies of the Press*, 9.

69. Ross, *Ladies of the Press*, xii.

70. Ross, *Ladies of the Press*, 3.

71. Ross, *Ladies of the Press*, 3.

72. Ross, *Ladies of the Press*, 23.

73. Sanders, *Dorothy Thompson*, 110–71.

74. Bent, "Personal Journalists," 4–5.

75. Bent, "Personal Journalists," 4–5.

76. *Time* Magazine, December 27, 1937, p. 49.

77. Alexander, "The Girl From Syracuse," 9–14.

78. Smith, "Herald Angel," 28.

79. Smith, "Herald Angel," 110.

80. Dalia Messick discussed the evolution of her long-running comic strip in an interview in the *Sacramento Bee*, January 22, 1992, Scene section, p. 1.

81. Marvel Cooke, interview by Kathleen Currie, 95–98, Women in Journalism Oral History Project of the Washington Press Club Foundation.

82. *California Eagle*, January 1, 1942, p. 1.

83. Bureau of the Census, *Sixteenth Census of the United States, 1940*: Labor Force, 3:75, 88.

84. Manning, *Ladies Now and Then*, 206.

85. Sorel, *Women Who Wrote the War*, xvi.

86. Gruber, *Ahead of Time*. Ruth Gruber, interview by author, May 1994.

87. Both Edwards, in *Women of the World*, and Sorel peg the number of accredited correspondents before the war at about 150 and the number accredited during the war at approximately 100. Sorel focuses on women's coverage of the growing conflict.

88. Bureau of the Census, *Seventeenth Census of the United States, 1950, Population*, 2:1–261, 1–276.

89. Sorel, *Women Who Wrote the War*, 182–83.

90. Sorel, *Women Who Wrote the War*, 183.

91. Ruth Cowan, interview by Margot Knight, September 1987, pp. 28–30, Women in Journalism Oral History Project of the Washington Press Club Foundation.

92. Helen Kirkpatrick, interview by Anne S. Kasper, April 3–5, 1990, Women in Journalism Oral History Project of the Washington Press Club Foundation, 36.

93. Sorel, *Women Who Wrote the War*, 219.

94. Helen Kirkpatrick, interview by Anne S. Kasper, 37, Women in Journalism Oral History Project of the Washington Press Club Foundation.

95. Helen Kirkpatrick, interview, 68–69, Women in Journalism Oral History Project of the Washington Press Club Foundation; Sorel, 204.

96. Higgins, *News Is a Singular Thing*, 39.

97. Higgins, *News Is a Singular Thing*, 46.

98. Higgins, *News Is a Singular Thing*, 89–97.

99. *Newsweek*, March 19, 1945, p. 88.

100. DeMar, "Negro Women Are Workers, Too," 72.

101. Two books look at the "Double V for Victory" program: Finkle, *Forum for Protest*, and Simmons, *The African American Press*.

102. *The New Republic*, April 26, 1943, pp. 557–60.

103. Bates, *Long Shadow of Little Rock*, 33–38.

104. McIntosh, "Girl Reporter," 47–55.

CHAPTER TWO: *Journey from the Star*

1. Radio interview with Ruth Finney, October 7, 1937, 1:51, Ruth Finney Papers.

2. Ross, *Ladies of the Press*, 340–42.

3. Finney diary, September 1922, 2:6, Ruth Finney Papers.

4. Finney diary, May 1930, 2:16, Ruth Finney Papers.

5. Finney diary, March 1937, 2:23, Ruth Finney Papers.

6. Journalistic pay figures are from Rosten, *The Washington Correspondents*, 185–89.

7. Finney diary, March 12, 1933, 2:19, Ruth Finney Papers.

8. Finney diary, March 1932, 2:18, Ruth Finney Papers.

9. "Journey from the Star," 1:4; Finney diary, December 3, 1924, 2:10, Ruth Finney Papers.

10. In her diary entry for February 14, 1929, Finney mentioned that she was traveling to Baltimore to see a "woman doctor," 2:15. She discusses the Mary Beard article in a February 1936 diary entry, 2:22, Ruth Finney Papers.

11. Finney diary, July 1928, 2:13, Ruth Finney Papers.

12. Finney diary, January 1929, 2:15, Ruth Finney Papers.

13. Finney diary, December 1935, 2:22, Ruth Finney Papers.

14. Finney titled her autobiography "Journey from the Star." The manuscript's subtitle was "Nice Work, And I Got It," 1:2, 51, Ruth Finney Papers.

15. "Journey from the Star," 1:2, 50, Ruth Finney Papers.

16. "Journey from the Star," 1:2, 15–44, Ruth Finney Papers.

17. "Journey from the Star," 1:2, 45–52, Ruth Finney Papers.

18. Finney diary, September 1918, 2:3, Ruth Finney Papers.

19. "Journey from the Star," 1:3, 63–70, Ruth Finney Papers.

20. "Journey from the Star," 1:3, 72–81, Ruth Finney Papers.

21. "Journey from the Star," 1:3, 77–83, Ruth Finney Papers.

22. Finney's stories on the Argonaut Mine disaster, 2:37, Ruth Finney Papers.

23. Finney's stories on the Argonaut Mine disaster, 2:37, Ruth Finney Papers.

24. Finney diary, August 1923, 2:7, Ruth Finney Papers.

25. The publication is not apparent, and the article is undated, but it is obviously from 1923 because Finney was still working in San Francisco; 2:60, Ruth Finney Papers.

26. Finney diary, September 17, 1922, 2:4, Ruth Finney Papers.

27. Finney diary, September 29, 1916, 2:2, Ruth Finney Papers.

28. Finney diary, February 2, 1917, 2:2, Ruth Finney Papers.

29. Finney short story, "To G. B. from B," 1:11, Ruth Finney Papers.

30. "Lady Boss" was written sometime in the 1930s or 1940s, 1:20, Ruth Finney Papers.

31. Finney diary, August 1918; October 1, 1918, 2:2; November 1920, 2:4, Ruth Finney Papers.

32. Finney diary, March 1932, 2:18, Ruth Finney Papers.

33. Finney describes her experiences at the Democratic convention in 1928 in "Journey from the Star," 1:5, 256, Ruth Finney Papers.

34. Finney diary, January 1923, 2:6, Ruth Finney Papers.

35. Finney diary, July 1923; September 4, 1923, 2:6, Ruth Finney Papers.

36. Finney diary, October 1923, 2:6, Ruth Finney Papers.

37. "Journey from the Star," 1:3, 146, Ruth Finney Papers.

38. "Journey from the Star," 1:4, 130–50, Ruth Finney Papers.

39. The long dispute over Boulder (later renamed Hoover) Dam is discussed in Moeller, *Phil Swing and Boulder Dam.*

40. "Journey from the Star," 1:5, 147–49, Ruth Finney Papers.

41. Finney diary, August 31, 1928, 2:13, Ruth Finney Papers.

42. "Journey from the Star," 1:5, 164, Ruth Finney Papers.

43. "Journey from the Star," 1:5, 174, Ruth Finney Papers.

44. "Journey from the Star," 1:5, 269–95, Ruth Finney Papers.

45. "Journey from the Star," 1:5, 296, Ruth Finney Papers.

46. *The Matrix* article is undated but probably appeared in 1927. An article from a paper called the *Argus* is from December 1927, but there is no mention of where the newspaper was published, 2:60, Ruth Finney Papers.

47. The story on Finney was written by Rodney Dutcher, a Scripps Howard reporter, and was syndicated in numerous publications. It appeared in several publications the week of December 28, 1927, 2:60, Ruth Finney Papers.

48. Furman, *Washington By-Line*, 44–45.

49. Hiram Johnson was a frequent Finney correspondent. He also sent notes and cards to her, declaring on one occasion that "my boss and I," meaning his wife, "give you our best," 3:2, Ruth Finney Papers.

50. California senator Hiram Johnson to Finney, August 27, 1927, 3:2, Ruth Finney Papers.

51. Finney diary, January 30, 1928; March 6, 1928; June 5, 1928; July 13, 1928, 2:13, Ruth Finney Papers.

52. Finney diary, December 14, 1928, 2:13; January 17, 1929, 2:14, Ruth Finney Papers.

53. Finney diary, November 1935, 2:21, Ruth Finney Papers.

54. Pilat, *Drew Pearson*, 115–26.

55. Finney diary, December 1931, 2:17, Ruth Finney Papers.

56. Finney diary, September 1936, 2:22, Ruth Finney Papers.

57. Finney diary, April 1936, 2:22; October 1933, 2:19, Ruth Finney Papers.

58. Finney diary, October 1933, 2:19, Ruth Finney Papers.

59. Finney diary, April 16, 1930, 2:16, Ruth Finney Papers.

60. Finney diary, March 1932, 2:18, Ruth Finney Papers.

61. Emery, Emery, and Roberts, *The Press and America*, 308–9.

62. Rosten, *Washington Correspondents*, 157.

63. Finney diary, July 1931, 2:17, Ruth Finney Papers.

64. Pilat, *Drew Pearson*, 116–17. Allen and Pearson claimed that, as a boy, Hoover had burned down his father's factory in Iowa. And they declared that he was not a great humanitarian, as he himself frequently claimed, rather he was vain and inept. These characterizations enraged the president, who sought to unearth the authors of *Washington Merry-Go-Round*.

65. Finney diary, August 1, 1932, 2:18, Ruth Finney Papers.

66. Finney diary, November 1932, 2:18, Ruth Finney Papers.

67. Finney diary, July 5, 1932, 2:18, Ruth Finney Papers.

68. "Journey from the Star," 1:5, 318–41, Ruth Finney Papers.

69. "Journey from the Star," 1:6, 366, Ruth Finney Papers.

70. Finney diary, March 12, 1933, 2:19, Ruth Finney Papers.

71. Beasley, *Eleanor Roosevelt and the Media*.

72. "Journey from the Star," 1:5, 365–70, Ruth Finney Papers.

73. "Journey from the Star," 1:5, 373, Ruth Finney Papers.

74. "Journey from the Star," 1:5, 375, Ruth Finney Papers.

75. Finney diary, July 1933, 2:19, Ruth Finney Papers.

76. Finney, *Careers for Women*.

77. Finney diary, January 1937, 2:23; "Journey from the Star," 1:7, 398–406, Ruth Finney Papers.

78. The series, titled "Portrait of a Modern Woman," appeared in dozens of papers across the country from May 28–June 3, 1937, 2:40, Ruth Finney Papers.

79. Finney diary, June 1937, 2:23, Ruth Finney Papers.

80. Finney diary, June 1940, 2:26, Ruth Finney Papers.

81. Finney diary, September 1937, 2:23, Ruth Finney Papers.

82. "Journey from the Star," 1:7, 452–61, Ruth Finney Papers.

83. "Journey from the Star," 1:7, 420–24, Ruth Finney Papers.

84. Finney diary, March 1934, 2:20, Ruth Finney Papers.

85. Finney diary, January 1936, 2:22; January 1937, 2:23, Ruth Finney Papers.

86. Finney diary, July 1941, 2:27, Ruth Finney Papers.

87. Finney diary, October 1940, 2:26, Ruth Finney Papers.

88. Finney diary, June 1941, 2:27, Ruth Finney Papers.

89. Finney diary, May 10, 1941; December 1941, 2:27, Ruth Finney Papers.

90. Finney diary, July 22, 1942, 2:28, Ruth Finney Papers.

91. Finney diary, July 22, 1942, 2:28, Ruth Finney Papers.

92. Stories on women defense plant workers appeared in papers across the country in August 1942, 2:58, Ruth Finney Papers.

93. Finney kept this obituary in a scrapbook filled with odds and ends, 3:18, Ruth Finney Papers.

94. Dinner comments are from November 10, 1947, 3:34, Ruth Finney Papers.

95. Managing editor's remarks are contained in a file of clippings about Finney, 2:60, Ruth Finney Papers.

96. The inscription carries only the initials C. E., 4:152, Ruth Finney Papers.

97. This obituary has no date, and no masthead identifies the newspaper. Robert Allen included it in her personal papers, 3:22, The Ruth Finney collection.

CHAPTER THREE: *The Press As Pulpit*

1. Bass, *Forty Years*, 16.

2. Finkle used the term "forum for protest" in his book of the same name, *Forum For Protest*.

3. hooks, *Ain't I a Woman*.

4. Giddings, *When and Where I Enter*, 7.

5. Collins, *Black Feminist Thought*, 92–94.

6. Smith, *Notable Black American Women*; Davis, *Contributions of Black Women*, 205–94.

7. Duster, *Crusade for Justice*, 33.

8. Wells discusses her life, career, and crusades on behalf of racial justice in her autobiography, *Crusade for Justice* (edited by Wells's daughter, Alfreda Duster, and published forty years after Wells's death).

9. Lewis discusses Wells's prickly and uncompromising personality in *W. E. B. DuBois*, 392–96. He specifically discusses her anger at being left off a list of committee members in the fledgling National Association for the Advancement of Colored People in 1909.

10. Duster, *Crusade for Justice*, 378.

11. Bass, *Forty Years*, 62.

12. Bass, *Forty Years*, 42.

13. *California Eagle*, August 25, 1930, p. 1.

14. Levy, *James Weldon Johnson*; Duberman, *Paul Robeson*; Lewis, *W. E. B. DuBois*.

15. Stein, *World of Marcus Garvey*, 170.

16. *Notable Black American Women* offers an October 1880 birth date and Sumter SC as her birthplace. The Los Angeles County death certificate lists Ohio as her birthplace. Records at Evergreen

Cemetery in Los Angeles, where Bass is buried, lists a February 14, 1874, birth date, and Ohio as her birthplace.

17. The school photo is probably from about 1890, and on the back, Bass or someone else wrote: "5 Afro-Americans in this class." (The Charlotta A. Bass Papers, MSS 022, Southern California Library for Social Studies and Research, 1:7. The collection contains date books, photos, copies of speeches, and a draft of her autobiography.)

18. Bass, *Forty Years*, 27.

19. Abajian, *Blacks and Their Contribution to the American West.*

20. Bass, *Forty Years*, 28.

21. de Graaf, *Negro Migration to Los Angeles*, 25–26. Also, Sonenshein, *Politics of Race and Power*, 22.

22. Sonenshein, *Politics of Race and Power*, 22.

23. Bureau of the Census, *Fourteenth Census of the United States, 1920*, 4:1129–30.

24. Bass, *Forty Years*, 28.

25. Bass, *Forty Years*, 31.

26. Bass, *Forty Years*, 31.

27. Danky, *African American Newspapers and Periodicals*, 606.

28. *California Eagle*, June 10, 1933, pp. 1–2.

29. Bass, *Forty Years*, 32.

30. Information on the breakdown of job categories between the Basses comes from Mary Tyler of the Southern California Library for Social Studies and Research, Los Angeles, which houses the Charlotta A. Bass Papers.

31. Bass, *Forty Years*, 31.

32. Bass, *Forty Years*, 35.

33. Bass, *Forty Years*, 41.

34. Bass, *Forty Years*, 43; Beasley, *Negro Trailblazers*, 255.

35. The paper's masthead carried her maiden name in conjunction with her husband's name until the mid-1920s, when she began using Bass exclusively.

36. Bass, *Forty Years*, 51–52.

37. *California Eagle*, February 18, 1922.

38. Tolbert, *UNIA and Black Los Angeles*, 41–45.

39. Bass, *Forty Years*, 57.

40. Bass, *Forty Years*, 59.

41. Streitmatter, *Raising Her Voice*, 99.

42. Prince, "A Sociological Analysis of the Negro Press in Los Angeles," 89–92.

43. Prince, "A Sociological Analysis of the Negro Press in Los Angeles," 89–92. California governor Edmund G. Brown Sr. appointed Loren Miller to the municipal court bench in the early 1960s.

44. *California Eagle*, April 17, 1930, p. 1.

45. *California Eagle*, October 23, 1931, p. 1.

46. *California Eagle*, June 30, 1933, p. 1.

47. *California Eagle*, April 21, 1933, p. 1.

48. Bass, *Forty Years*, p. 67.

49. *California Eagle*, December 8, 1938, p. 1.

50. Leonard, "Years of Hope, Days of Fear," 37–40; de Graaf, 21–22, 79–81.

51. *California Eagle*, May 18, 1933, p. 1.

52. *California Eagle*, January 26, 1934, p. 1.

53. *California Eagle*, February 2, 1934, p. 1.

54. Bass, *Forty Years*, 81–82.

55. *California Eagle*, May 6, 1931, p. 4.

56. *California Eagle*, September 18, 1931, p. 1.

57. *California Eagle*, April 17, 1931, p. 1.

58. *California Eagle*, February 10, 1944, p. 5.

59. *California Eagle*, July 1931–February 1933.

60. *California Eagle*, February 23, 1934, p. 1.

61. *California Eagle*, February 2, 1939, p. 1

62. *California Eagle*, November 3, 1938, p. 1.

63. *California Eagle*, December 7, 1939, p. 6.

64. Bogle, *Dorothy Dandridge*, 133.

65. *California Eagle*, November 30, 1939, p. 1.

66. *California Eagle*, July 7, 1941, p. 1.

67. *California Eagle*, January 15, 1942, p. 1.

68. *California Eagle*, December 12, 1941, p. 5.

69. *California Eagle*, September 24, 1942, p. 1.

70. Bass, *Forty Years*, 96.

71. Bass, *Forty Years*, 109–11.

72. Information about the FBI and black newspapers in World War II is contained in Finkle, *Forum for Protest*, and in Washburn, "J. Edgar Hoover and the Black Press in World War II," 26–32.

73. *California Eagle*, January 12, 1939, p. 1.

74. Bass, *Forty Years*, 123.

75. *California Eagle*, January 18, 1945, p. 1.

76. *California Eagle*, January 18, 1945, p. 1.

77. *California Eagle*, April 5, 1945, p. 1.

78. This quote appears in Bass's acceptance speech as vice presidential candidate for the Independent Progressive Party in 1952, 2:10, Charlotta A. Bass Papers.

79. *California Eagle*, February 20 1947, p. 5.

80. McWhorter, *Carry Me Home*, 62.

81. Barrett, *The Tenney Committee*, vol. 17. See also *Report: Joint Fact-Finding Committee on Un-American Activities in California*, published by the Senate of the State of California, 1945, 28:4113–31. The committee listed numerous communist-inspired groups that Bass belonged to, including the International Committee on African Affairs, the International Labor Defense, and American Youth for Democracy. It also noted her friendships with Paul Robeson and civil rights activist Carey McWilliams.

82. Bass, *Forty Years*, 178–79.

83. *Time* Magazine, March 17, 1952, p. 20.

84. 1:18, Charlotta A. Bass Papers.

CHAPTER FOUR: *Murder Was Her Beat*

1. *Los Angeles Evening Herald and Express*, October 27, 1936, C4–5.

2. Underwood, *Newspaperwoman*, 94.

3. Underwood, *Newspaperwoman*, 1.

4. Underwood, *Newspaperwoman*, 103.

5. Underwood, *Newspaperwoman*, 9.

6. Hubbard Keavy, "Aggie Underwood, A Profile of the Legendary Lady City Editor of the Los Angeles Herald-Express," *Air California*, July 1975, pp. 18–25, 1:10, Agness M. Underwood Collection.

7. Underwood, *Newspaperwoman*, 112.

8. Jack Smith, interview by author, October 1993. Smith worked with Underwood at the *Herald and Express* before moving on to the

Los Angeles Times, where he worked as a columnist until his death in 1998.

9. Underwood, *Newspaperwoman,* 2.

10. Underwood, *Newspaperwoman,* 18.

11. Underwood, *Newspaperwoman,* 24.

12. Underwood, *Newspaperwoman,* 16.

13. Underwood, *Newspaperwoman,* 16–26.

14. Underwood, *Newspaperwoman,* 27.

15. Underwood, *Newspaperwoman,* 15.

16. Underwood, *Newspaperwoman,* 32.

17. Underwood, *Newspaperwoman,* 3–4.

18. Underwood, *Newspaperwoman,* 3.

19. Underwood, *Newspaperwoman,* 2.

20. Underwood, *Newspaperwoman,* 2–3.

21. Underwood, *Newspaperwoman,* 4.

22. Underwood, *Newspaperwoman,* 237.

23. Speech given by Underwood to a San Francisco Press Club gathering honoring student journalists, April 29, 1950, Box AMU, A/V, Agness M. Underwood Collection.

24. George Underwood, interview by author, telephone, October 30–November 1, 1994.

25. Underwood, *Newspaperwoman,* 38.

26. Underwood, *Newspaperwoman,* 40.

27. Underwood, *Newspaperwoman,* 41.

28. Underwood, *Newspaperwoman,* 42.

29. Underwood, *Newspaperwoman,* 43.

30. Interview, 1:21, Agness M. Underwood Collection.

31. Underwood, *Newspaperwoman,* 43.

32. Author interviews with Jack Smith, October 1993, and Vi Phillips, October 1994, whose husband Ed Phillips worked with Underwood. Both remembered that she remained good friends with Harry Underwood and that she never married again.

33. George Underwood, interview by author, telephone, November 30, 1994.

34. Underwood, *Newspaperwoman,* 45.

35. Underwood, *Newspaperwoman,* 46.

36. Underwood, *Newspaperwoman,* 50.

37. Underwood, *Newspaperwoman*, 58.

38. Underwood, *Newspaperwoman*, 65.

39. Underwood, *Newspaperwoman*, 79.

40. Agness Underwood, interviewed by Tom Reilly, Box AMU, A/ V, Agness M. Underwood Collection.

41. Underwood, *Newspaperwoman*, 103.

42. *Los Angeles Evening Herald and Express*, January 4, 1936, p. 1; June 28, 1936, p. 1.

43. Underwood, *Newspaperwoman*, 128.

44. *Los Angeles Evening Herald and Express*, March 19, 1936, p. 1.

45. *Los Angeles Evening Herald and Express*, April 1, 1935, p. 3.

46. *Los Angeles Evening Herald and Express*, April 3, 1935, p. 3.

47. *Los Angeles Evening Herald and Express*, March 30, 1935, p. 3.

48. Underwood, *Newspaperwoman*, 153.

49. Underwood, *Newspaperwoman*, 88–89.

50. *Los Angeles Evening Herald and Express*, January 15, 1936, p. 1.

51. *Los Angeles Evening Herald and Express*, March 2, 1936, p. 1.

52. *Los Angeles Times*, March 6, 1936, p. 2.

53. *Los Angeles Evening Herald and Express*, April 2, 1936, p. A2.

54. *Newsweek*, March 24, 1947, p. 67.

55. Underwood, *Newspaperwoman*, 162.

56. Underwood, *Newspaperwoman*, 248.

57. Underwood, *Newspaperwoman*, 222.

58. Underwood, *Newspaperwoman*, 181.

59. Underwood, *Newspaperwoman*, 181.

60. Wolf and Mader, *Fallen Angels*, 165–72.

61. *Los Angeles Evening Herald and Express*, December 22, 1944, p. 1.

62. Underwood, *Newspaperwoman*, 149–50.

63. *Los Angeles Times*, May 22, 1945, p. 1. Peete's trial filled the front pages of the *Los Angeles Evening Herald and Express* from May 9–28, 1945, when she was convicted.

64. Underwood, *Newspaperwoman*, 149.

65. Underwood, *Newspaperwoman*, 151.

66. *Los Angeles Times*, May 29, 1945, p. 1. Peete became only the second woman executed in California, in April 1947.

67. Underwood, *Newspaperwoman*, 6.

68. Underwood, *Newspaperwoman*, 8.

69. *Time* Magazine, June 30, 1947, p. 62.

70. *Newsweek*, March 24, 1947, p. 67.

71. *Newsweek*, March 24, 1947, p. 67.

72. Underwood, *Newspaperwoman*, p. 292.

73. Underwood, *Newspaperwoman*, 281.

74. Underwood, *Newspaperwoman*, 281.

75. Underwood, *Newspaperwoman*, 284.

76. Jack Smith, interview by author, October 1993.

77. *The American Policeman*, July 1948, p. 1.

78. Winchell speech, June 20, 1958, 4:24, Agness M. Underwood Collection.

79. Cott used the expression "group called women" in *Grounding of Modern Feminism*, 5.

80. Underwood was interviewed in 1976 by Natalie Holtzman who was completing a master's degree in journalism at California State University, Northridge. Holtzman suggested that Underwood could be considered a role model for second-wave feminists, and Underwood did not disagree. Audiotape, Box AMU A/V, Agness M. Underwood Collection.

Afterword

1. Mandel, *Modern Journalism*, 271–76.

2. McClendon, *My Eight Presidents* 49, 168.

3. Thomas, *Dateline*, xviii.

4. Robertson, *Girls in the Balcony*, 99.

5. Robertson, *Girls in the Balcony*, 74.

6. Helen Thomas, interview by author, California State University, Sacramento, March 11, 1999.

7. Friedan, *Feminine Mystique*, 74.

8. Davis, *Contributions of Black Women*, 260–61. Others have also written about Dunnigan, including Streitmatter, "Alice Allison Dunnigan" 87–97.

9. Payne, interview by Kathleen Currie, Women in Journalism Oral History Project of the Washington Press Club Foundation, September 8, 1987, 46.

10. Payne, interview by Kathleen Currie, Women in Journalism Oral History Project of the Washington Press Club Foundation, September 8, 1987, 41.

11. The author was among those young women journalists of the 1980s, who were stunned that someone from Underwood's generation could have succeeded at this level.

Bibliography

Manuscript Collections

Agness M. Underwood Collection. Urban Archives Center, California State University, Northridge.

Charlotta A. Bass Papers. MSS 022, Southern California Library for Social Studies and Research, Los Angeles.

Ruth Finney Papers. D-70, Department of Special Collections, General Library, University of California, Davis.

Women in Journalism Oral History Project of the Washington Press Club Foundation. Columbia University, New York.

Published Sources

Abajian, James de T. *Blacks and Their Contributions to the American West: A Bibliography and Union List of Library Holdings through 1970.* Boston: G. K. Hall & Co., 1974.

Alexander, Jack. "The Girl From Syracuse, the Story of Problem Child Dorothy Thompson," *Saturday Evening Post,* May 18, 1940, pp. 9–14.

Alpern, Sara. *Freda Kirchwey, A Woman of the Nation.* Cambridge: Harvard University Press, 1987.

Antler, Joyce. "Feminism as Life-Process: The Life and Career of Lucy Sprague Mitchell." *Feminist Studies* 7 (1981): 134–51.

Barrett, Edward L. Jr. *The Tenney Committee: Legislative Investigation of Subversive Activities in California.* Ithaca: Cornell University Press, 1951.

Barth, Gunther. "Metropolitan Press." *City People: The Rise of Modern City Culture in Nineteenth-Century America.* New York: Oxford University Press, 1980.

Basinger, Jeanine. *A Woman's View: How Hollywood Spoke to Women, 1930–1960.* New York: Alfred A. Knopf, 1993.

Bass, Charlotta. *Forty Years: Memoirs from the Pages of a Newspaper*. Los Angeles: Charlotta Bass, 1960.

Bates, Daisy. *The Long Shadow of Little Rock*. Fayetteville: University of Arkansas Press, 1987.

Beasley, Delilah. *Negro Trailblazers of California*. Los Angeles: Delilah Beasley, 1919.

Beasley, Maurine. *Eleanor Roosevelt and the Media: A Public Quest for Self-Fulfillment*. Champaign: University of Illinois Press, 1987.

——"Mary Marvin Breckenridge Patterson, Case Study of One of 'Murrow's Boys.'" *Journalism History* 20 (1994): 25–33.

——"Women in Journalism Education: The Formative Period, 1908–1930." *Journalism History* 13 (1986): 10–19.

——"The Women's National Press Club: Case Study of Professional Aspirations." *Journalism History* 15 (1988): 112–21.

Bennion, Sherilyn Cox. *Equal to the Occasion: Women Editors of the Nineteenth-Century West*. Reno: University of Nevada Press, 1990.

Bent, Silas. "Personal Journalists," *The Saturday Review of Literature*, December 12, 1936, pp. 4–5

Bessie, Simon. *Jazz Journalism*. New York: Russell and Russell, 1938.

Bogle, Donald. *Dorothy Dandridge*. New York: Amistad, 1997.

Bolin, Winifred D. Wandersee. "The Economics of Middle-Income Family Life: Working Women during the Great Depression." *Journal of American History* 65 (1978): 60–74.

Bourke-White, Margaret. *Portrait of Myself*. New York: Simon & Schuster, 1963.

Brady, Kathleen. *Ida Tarbell: Portrait of a Muckraker*. New York: Seaview/Putnam, 1984.

Brody, Catharine. "Newspaper Girls," *American Mercury*, March 1926, pp. 273–76.

Bureau of the Census. *Fifteen Census of the United States, 1930*. Vol. 5: *General Report on Occupations*. Washington DC, 1934.

Bureau of the Census. *Seventeenth Census of the United States, 1950*. Vol. 2: *Population*. Washington DC, 1952.

Bureau of the Census. *Sixteenth Census of the United States, 1940*. Vol. 3: *The Labor Force*. Washington DC: GPO, 1943.

Bureau of the Census. *U.S. Census of Population, 1950.* Vol. 2: *Characteristics of the Population.* Washington DC: GPO, 1953.

Caswell, Lucy Shelton. "Edwina Dumm: Pioneer Woman Editorial Cartoonist, 1915–1917." *Journalism History* 15 (1988): 2–6.

Chafe, William. *The Paradox of Change: American Women in the Twentieth-Century.* New York: Oxford University Press, 1991.

Cheshire, Maxine, and John Greenya. *Maxine Cheshire, Reporter.* Boston: Houghton Mifflin, 1978.

Collins, Patricia Hill. *Black Feminist Thought: Knowledge, Consciousness and the Politics of Empowerment.* Boston: Unwin Hyman, 1990.

Cook, Blanche Weisen. *Eleanor Roosevelt,* vol. 2. New York: Viking, 1999.

Cott, Nancy. *The Grounding of Modern Feminism.* New Haven: Yale University Press, 1987.

Danky, James. *African-American Newspapers and Periodicals: A National Bibliography.* Cambridge: Harvard University Press, 1999.

Davis, Mariana, ed. *Contributions of Black Women to America,* vol. 1. Columbia SC: Kenday Press, Inc., 1982.

de Graaf, Lawrence Brooks. *Negro Migration to Los Angeles, 1930–1950.* San Francisco: R and E Research Associates, 1974.

DeMar, George. "Negro Women Are Workers, Too," *Opportunity,* April 1943, 72.

Dick, Bernard. *Radical Innocence: A Critical Study of the Hollywood Ten.* Lexington: University Press of Kentucky, 1989.

Dorr, Rheta Childe. *A Woman of Fifty.* New York: Funk and Wagnalls, 1924.

Duberman, Martin. *Paul Robeson.* New York: Knopf, 1988.

DuBois, Ellen Carol, and Vicki L. Ruiz, eds. *Unequal Sisters: A Multi-Cultural Reader in U.S. Women's History.* New York: Routledge, 1990.

Dunnigan, Alice. "Early History of Negro Women in Journalism." *The Negro History Bulletin* 28 (1966): 178–79, 193, 197.

Duster, Alfreda M., ed. *Crusade for Justice: The Autobiography of Ida B. Wells.* Chicago: The University of Chicago Press, 1970.

Echols, Alice. *Daring to be Bad: Radical Feminism in America, 1967–75* Minneapolis: University of Minnesota Press, 1989.

Edwards, Julia. *Women of the World: The Great Foreign Correspondents*. New York: Ballantine Books, 1988.

Emery, Michael, Edwin Emery, and Nancy Roberts. *The Press and America: An Interpretative History of Mass Media*. Boston: Allyn and Bacon, 2000.

Faber, Doris. *The Life of Lorena Hickok: E. R.'s Friend*. New York: William Morrow & Co., 1980.

Fass, Paula. *The Damned and the Beautiful: American Youth in the 1920s*. New York: Oxford University Press, 1977.

Filene, Catherine, ed. *Careers for Women: New Ideas, New Methods, New Opportunities*. Boston: Houghton Mifflin, 1934.

Finkle, Lee. *Forum for Protest: The Black Press during World War II*. Cranbury NJ: Associated University Presses, Inc., 1975.

Finney, Ruth. "The Reporter." *Careers for Women: New Ideas, New Methods, New Opportunities*. Boston: Houghton Mifflin, 1934.

Fleischman, Doris E., ed. *Outline of Careers for Women: A Practical Guide to Achievement*. New York: Doubleday, Doran & Company, Inc., 1931.

Freedman, Estelle. "The New Woman: Changing Views of Women in the 1920s." *Journal of American History* 61 (1974): 372–393.

Friedan, Betty. *The Feminine Mystique*. New York: Dell Publishing, 1963.

Furman, Bess. *Washington By-Line: The Personal History of a Newspaperwoman*. New York: Alfred A. Knopf, 1949.

Galerstein, Carolyn. *Working Women on the Hollywood Screen: A Filmography*. New York: Garland Publishing, 1989.

Gellhorn, Martha. *The Trouble I've Seen*. New York: William Morrow & Co., 1936.

Giddings, Paula. *When and Where I Enter: The Impact of Black Women on Race and Sex in America*. New York: W. Morrow, 1984.

Gilman, Mildred. *Sob Sister*. New York: Jonathan Cape and Harrison Smith, 1931.

Goodwin, Doris Kearns. *No Ordinary Time: Franklin and Eleanor Roosevelt: The Home Front in World War II*. New York: Simon & Schuster, 1994.

Gottlieb, Agnes Hooper. "Networking in the Nineteenth Century:

The Founding of the Women's Press Club of New York City."
Journalism History 21 (1995): 156–63.

Gottlieb, Robert, and Irene Wolt. *Thinking Big: The Story of the Los Angeles Times, Its Publishers, and Their Influence on Southern California.* New York: G. P. Putnam's Sons, 1977.

Grant, Judith. *Fundamental Feminism: Contesting the Core Concepts of Feminist Theory.* New York: Routledge, 1993.

Gruber, Ruth. *Ahead of Time: My Early Years as a Foreign Correspondent.* New York: Wynwood Press, 1994.

Harris, Barbara. *Beyond Her Sphere: Women and the Professions in American History.* Westport CT: Greenwood Press, 1978.

Haskell, Molly. *From Reverence to Rape: The Treatment of Women in the Movies.* Chicago: University of Chicago Press, 1973.

Heald, Morrell. *Transatlantic Vistas: American Journalists in Europe, 1900–1940.* Columbus: Ohio State University Press, 1988.

Hertzberg, Joseph. *Late City Edition.* New York: Archon Books, 1947.

Higgins, Marguerite. *News is a Singular Thing.* Garden City NJ: Doubleday & Co., 1955.

Hill, Joseph A. *Women in Gainful Occupations, 1870–1920.* Census Monographs IX. Washington DC: GPO, 1929.

Hohenberg, John. *Foreign Correspondence: The Great Reporters and Their Times.* New York: Columbia University Press, 1964.

hooks, bell. *Ain't I a Woman: Black Women and Feminism.* Boston: South End Press, 1981.

Horn, Maurice. *Women in the Comics.* New York: Chelsea House Publishers, 1977.

Hosley, David, and Gayle Yamada. *Hard News: Women in Broadcast Journalism.* Westport CT: Greenwood Press, 1987.

Jackson, Luther. "The Popular Media: Part I, The Mission of Black Newsmen." *The Black American Reference Book.* Englewood Cliffs NJ: Prentice-Hall, 1976.

Jones, Jacqueline. *Labor of Love, Labor of Sorrow: Black Women, Work, and the Family from Slavery to the Present.* New York: Basic Books, 1985.

Juergens, George. *Joseph Pulitzer and the New York World.* Princeton: Princeton University Press, 1966.

Kael, Pauline. *The Citizen Kane Book: Raising Kane.* Boston: Little, Brown & Company, 1971.

Kelly, Florence Finch. *Flowing Stream: The Story of Fifty-Six Years in American Newspaper Life*. New York: E. P. Dutton & Co., Inc., 1939.

Kessler-Harris, Alice. *In Pursuit of Equity: Women, Men, and the Quest for Economic Citizenship in 20th-Century America*. Oxford: Oxford University Press, 2001.

——*Out to Work: A History of Wage-Earning Women in the United States*. New York: Oxford University Press, 1982.

Klehr, Harvey. *The Heyday of American Communism: The Depression Decade*. New York: Basic Books, 1984.

Kluger, Richard. *The Paper: The Life and Death of the New York Herald Tribune*. New York: Alfred A. Knopf, 1986.

Kroeger, Brooke. *Nellie Bly: Daredevil, Reporter, Feminist*. New York: Random House, 1994.

Langer, Elinor. *Josephine Herbst*. Boston: Little, Brown & Company, 1983.

Lemons, J. Stanley. *The Woman Citizen: Social Feminism in the 1920s*. Champaign: University of Illinois Press, 1973.

Leonard, Kevin. "Years of Hope, Days of Fear: The Impact of World War II on Race Relations in Los Angeles." Ph.D. diss., University of California, Davis, 1992.

Lerner, Gerda, ed. *Black Women in White America: A Documentary History*. New York: Vintage Books, 1972.

Leuck, Mariam Simons. *Fields of Work for Women*. New York: D. Appleton-Century Company, 1938.

Levy, Eugene. *James Weldon Johnson: Black Leader, Black Voice*. Chicago: University of Chicago Press, 1973.

Lewis, David Levering. *W. E. B. DuBois, Biography of a Race*. New York: Henry Holt, 1993.

Lipsitz, George. *Time Passages: Collective Memory and American Popular Culture*. Minneapolis: University of Minnesota Press, 1990.

Logie, Iona Robertson. *Careers for Women in Journalism: A Composite Picture of Salaried Women Writers at Work in Journalism, Advertising, Publicity, and Promotion*. Scranton PA: International Textbook Publishing, 1941.

Lowell, Joan. *Gal Reporter*. New York: Farrar & Rinehart, 1933.

Mandel, Siegfried, ed. *Modern Journalism*. New York: Pitman Publishing Corp., 1962.

Manning, Marie. *Ladies Now and Then.* New York: E. P. Dutton & Co., 1944.

Marbut, F. B. *News From the Capitol: The Story of Washington Reporting.* Carbondale: Southern Illinois University Press, 1971.

Marchand, Roland. *Advertising the American Dream: Making Way for Modernity 1920–1940.* Berkeley: University of California Press, 1982.

Martin, Ralph. *Cissy: The Extraordinary Life of Eleanor Medill Patterson.* New York: Simon & Schuster, 1979.

Marzolf, Marion. *Up from the Footnote: A History of Women Journalists.* New York: Hastings House, 1977.

May, Antoinette. *Witness to War: A Biography of Marguerite Higgins.* New York: Beaufort Books, Inc., 1983.

May, Elaine Tyler. *Homeward Bound: American Families in the Cold War Era.* New York: Basic Books, 1988.

McBride, Joseph. *Hawks On Hawks.* Berkeley: University of California Press, 1982.

McBride, Mary Margaret. *A Long Way from Missouri.* New York: G. P. Putnam's Sons, 1959.

McClendon, Sarah. *My Eight Presidents.* New York: Wyden Books, 1978.

McGlashan, Zena Beth. "Club 'Ladies' and Working 'Girls'": Rheta Childe Dorr and the *New York Evening Post.*" *Journalism History* 8 (1981): 7–13.

——"Women Witness the Russian Revolution: Analyzing Ways of Seeing." *Journalism History* 12 (1985): 54–61.

McIntosh, India. "Girl Reporter." *Late City Edition.* New York: Archon Books, 1947.

McWhorter, Diane. *Carry Me Home, Birmingham, Alabama: The Climactic Battle of the Civil Rights Revolution.* New York: Simon & Schuster, 2001.

Merrick, Beverly. "Mary Margaret McBride: At Home in Hudson Valley," *Journalism History* 22 (1996): 110–18.

Mills, Kay. *A Place in the News: From the Women's Pages to the Front Page.* New York: Columbia University Press, 1990.

Moeller, Beverley Bowen. *Phil Swing and Boulder Dam.* Berkeley: University of California Press, 1971.

Morantz-Sanchez, Regina Markel. *Sympathy and Science: Women Physicians in American Medicine.* New York: Oxford University Press, 1985.

Mott, Frank Luther. *American Journalism: A History of Newspapers in the United States through 260 Years: 1690 to 1950.* New York: MacMillan Company, 1950.

Oglesby, Catharine. "Women in Journalism," *Ladies Home Journal,* May 29, 1930, p. 29.

O'Neill, William. *Everyone Was Brave: A History of Feminism in America.* Chicago: Quadrangle Books, 1969.

Ostroff, Roberta. *Fire in the Wind: The Life of Dickey Chapelle.* New York: Ballantine Books, 1992.

Pilat, Oliver. *Drew Pearson: An Unauthorized Biography.* New York: Harper's Magazine Press, 1973.

Prince, Virginia Ann. "A Sociological Analysis of the Negro Press in Los Angeles." Master's thesis, University of Southern California, 1946.

Robertson, Nan. *Girls in the Balcony: Women, Men, and the "New York Times."* New York: Random House, 1992.

Rollyson, Carl. *Nothing Ever Happens to the Brave: The Story of Martha Gellhorn.* New York: St. Martin's Press, 1990.

Rosen, Marjorie. *Popcorn Venus: Women, Movies, and the American Dream.* New York: Coward, McCann, and Geoghegan, 1973.

Rosenberg, Rosalind. *Beyond Separate Spheres: Intellectual Roots of Modern Feminism.* New Haven: Yale University Press, 1982.

Ross, Ishbel. *Ladies of the Press: The Story of Women in Journalism by an Insider.* New York: Harper & Bros., 1936.

Rosten, Leo. *The Washington Correspondents.* New York: Arno Press, 1974.

Sanders, Marion K. *Dorothy Thompson: A Legend in Her Time.* Boston: Houghton Mifflin, 1973.

Scharf, Lois. *To Work and To Wed: Female Employment, Feminism, and the Great Depression.* Westport CT: Greenwood Press, 1980.

Schudson, Michael. *Discovering the News: A Social History of American Journalism.* New York: Basic Books, 1978.

Scott, Joan. *Gender and the Politics of History.* New York: Columbia University Press, 1988.

Shilpp, Madelon Golden, and Sharon M. Murphy. *Great Women of the Press*. Carbondale: Southern Illinois University Press, 1983.

Simmons, Charles A. *The African American Press: A History of News Coverage during National Crises, with Special Reference to Four Black Newspapers, 1827–1965*. Jefferson NC: McFarland & Co., Inc., 1998.

Sklar, Robert. *Movie-Made America: A Social History of American Movies*. New York: Random House, 1975.

Smith, Beverly. "Herald Angel," *The American Magazine*, August, 1940, p. 28

Smith, Jessie Carney, ed. *Notable Black American Women*. Detroit: Gale Research, 1992.

Smith, Wilda M., and Eleanor A. Bogart. *The Wars of Peggy Hull: The Life and Times of a War Correspondent*. El Paso: Texas Western Press, 1991.

Smythe, Mabel, ed. *The Black American Reference Book*. Englewood Cliffs NJ: Prentice Hall, Inc., 1976.

Sonenshein, Raphael J. *Politics of Race and Power in Los Angeles*. Princeton: Princeton University Press, 1993.

Sorel, Nancy Caldwell. *The Women Who Wrote the War*. New York: Arcade Publishing, 1999.

Stein, Judith. *The World of Marcus Garvey*. Baton Rouge: Louisiana State University Press, 1986.

Steiner, Linda, and Susanne Gray. "Autobiographies by Women Journalists: An Annotated Bibliography." *Journalism History* 23 (1997): 13–15.

——"Genevieve Forbes Herrick: A Front Page Reporter 'Pleased to Write About Women.'" *Journalism History* 12 (1985): 8–16.

Sterling, Dorothy. *Black Foremothers: Three Lives*. New York: Feminist Press, 1988.

St. Johns, Adela Rogers. *The Honeycomb*. New York: Doubleday and Company, 1969.

Streitmatter, Rodger. "Alice Allison Dunnigan: An African-American Woman Journalist Who Broke a Double Barrier." *Journalism History* 16 (1989): 87–97.

——*Raising Her Voice: African American Women Journalists Who Changed History*. Lexington: University Press of Kentucky, 1994.

Stricker, Frank. "Cookbooks and Law Books: The Hidden History of Career Women in Twentieth-Century America." *Journal of Social History* 10 (1976): 1–19.

Strong, Tracy B., and Helene Keyssar. *Right in Her Soul: The Life of Anna Louise Strong.* New York: Random House, 1983.

Swanberg, W. A. *Citizen Hearst: A Biography of William Randolph Hearst.* New York: Charles Scribner's Sons, 1961.

Talese, Gay. *The Kingdom and the Power.* New York: World Publishing, 1969.

Tarry, Ellen. *The Third Door: The Autobiography of an American Negro Woman.* New York: McKay, 1955.

Terborg-Penn, Rosalyn, and Sharon Harley, eds. *The Afro-American Woman: Struggles and Images.* Port Washington NY: Kennikat Press, 1978.

Thomas, Helen. *Dateline: White House.* New York: MacMillan, 1975.

Thompson, Dorothy. "Women Correspondents and Other New Ideas," *The Nation,* January 6, 1926, pp. 11–12.

Tolbert, Emory. *The UNIA and Black Los Angeles.* Edina MN: Bellwether Press, 1989.

Toll, Robert. *The Entertainment Machine.* New York: Oxford University Press, 1982.

Underwood, Agness. *Newspaperwoman.* New York: Harper and Brothers, 1949.

U.S. Congress. *Official Congressional Directory,* 68th–80th Cong., Session 1, May 1924–June 1947.

Walker, Stanley. *City Editor.* New York: Frederick A. Stokes Co., 1934.

——"A City Editor's Testament," *The American Mercury,* September 1931, pp. 25–34.

Waller, Mary Ellen. "Vera Connolly: Progressive Journalist." *Journalism History* 15 (1988): 80–89.

Ware, Susan. *Holding Their Own: American Women in the 1930s.* Boston: Twayne Publishing, 1982.

——*Still Missing: Amelia Earhart and the Search for Modern Feminism.* New York: W. W. Norton, 1993.

Washburn, Patrick S. "J. Edgar Hoover and the Black Press in World War II." *Journalism History* 13 (1986): 26–33.

Weiner, Lynn. *From Working Girl to Working Mother: The Female La-*

bor Force in the United States, 1820–1980. Chapel Hill: University of North Carolina Press, 1985.

Weisbrot, Robert. *Freedom Bound: A History of America's Civil Rights Movement.* New York: Norton, 1990.

Wolf, Marvin J., and Katherine Mader. *Fallen Angels: Chronicles of L.A. Crime and Mystery.* New York: Facts on File Publications, 1986.

Woloch, Nancy, *Women and the American Experience.* New York: Alfred A. Knopf, 1984.

CPSIA information can be obtained
at www.ICGtesting.com
Printed in the USA
LVHW080840170321
681697LV00024B/1530